DIPLOMATIC CHANNELS

By the same author

THE MIDDLE EAST IN REVOLUTION

LIVING WITH THE COMMUNISTS

THE INDIA WE LEFT

DIPLOMATIC CHANNELS

Humphrey Trevelyan

Gambit
INCORPORATED
Boston
1973

First printing

Copyright © 1973 by Lord Trevelyan

Library of Congress Catalog Card Number: 73–81316
International Standard Book Number: 0–87645–080–X
Printed in the United States of America

Contents

5

'In far lodgings east and west
Lie down on the beds you made.'

A. E. Housman, *Last Poems*

Preface

My generation in the British foreign service, now known as the diplomatic service, witnessed the diminution of British power, caused by the immense growth in economic and therefore in military and political power of the United States of America and the Soviet Union. In the decade after the war the British were still in the top class. We were one of the great states engaged in the peace settlement and had our own zone of occupation in Germany. We shared the secrets of the early atomic bomb, to which we had made a major contribution. We had played a principal part in shaping the United Nations. We had a special position in the Middle East and colonies in Africa, though India had gone. We led the commonwealth in practice as well as in theory. We basked in the afterglow of victory, and still felt secure in our own right.

Now that time is over. We are a European state, limited in size and power. We have virtually withdrawn from east of Suez and the Middle East and have given independence to nearly all our colonies. India, so recently ruled from King Charles street, has signed a treaty of friendship with the Soviet Union which gives it, at least on paper, a privileged status. Our special relationship with the United States no longer exists. Our economic strength is surpassed by Germany and Japan and our standard of living is falling back in the league table. We have just entered the European community, most of us having belatedly recognised that this is now our proper rôle in the world. We have to adapt our diplomacy to the new environment, a world of rapid change, dominated by the super-powers, racked by violence and torn by the dissensions of ideology and race, in which a multitude of new states, having thrown off the harness and convenience of foreign domination, grope their way towards an uncertain future, beset by internal and external rivalries, poverty and backwardness.

In these conditions, in the short span of a few decades, the world of diplomacy and the life of the diplomat, especially of the British diplomat, have markedly changed, though the principles of diplomacy remain essentially the same. I have tried to describe what the practice of diplomacy and the diplomat's life is like in these days. What I have written is not a diplomatic memoir, though I have drawn liberally on my own experience since 1947, the year when my life in India was cut short by Indian independence and I was received from the Indian into the welcoming and charitable arms of the British service. It might be described as a precocious child's guide to diplomacy. It is not meant for the serious student nor for the seasoned professionals. It will not help anyone to pass an examination in modern politics. Nor is it an official view, as you will surely see if you read on. If I am bold enough to suggest a few simple direction posts for those engaged in the profession, I do not claim to have observed them correctly myself.

I am concerned with diplomats and governments in general, though there is a British flavour. I hope that the views which I express do not foul the diplomatic nest which protected me for so long from the sharp winds of competitive life, and that they reflect in a properly objective manner my admiration for my old service which successfully adapts itself to changing conditions and changing British interests. Having a lively sympathy for those ladies who incautiously married into the diplomatic service and found themselves continually propelled round the continents, I take the opportunity to pay my tribute to one of them, my long-suffering wife, who shared the diplomatic life with me, largely contributing to any good I have done in it, and who endured its trials and tribulations with grace and without complaint.

There are a few passages which echo what I have written in my accounts of the situations in which I found myself in the Middle East, China and the Soviet Union. For this I apologise to the readers, if there are any, who have stayed the full course. Some duplication is inevitable if I am to cover the ground. With reluctance I have used the word 'diplomat', which has now, to the disgust of those who have been properly brought up, crossed the Channel and effectively replaced the more correct but slightly pompous 'diplomatist'. I have also generally used the name 'foreign office' for the British ministry of external affairs, since that was its name in my time and the correct name of the moment, 'foreign and commonwealth office', is more of a mouthful. I am grateful to two members of the British service and to Mr Handasyde Buchanan who have been kind enough to read the manuscript and make pertinent suggestions.

I wanted to call this book *Envoys ordinary*, which is what it is about; but Macmillan's would not have it, and my only means of retaliation is to add this sentence to the preface. I daresay the present, more prosaic title expresses its scope well enough.

One

The Career

The average citizen, with his eyes glued to the 'box', has only the vaguest idea what an ambassador does. In the press he is pictured standing by a carriage from the royal or presidential palace with his chest covered in gold lace or in evening dress in the middle of the morning, splashed with orders and decorations like an old-fashioned swimming instructor. In Osbert Lancaster's cartoons his white tie and broad sash are accompanied by the paunch and debilitated look of one whom the restrictions of his profession have required to make do for vices with an excess of food, drink and sleep. Questions in parliament suggest that he is solely occupied in giving extravagant parties at the taxpayer's expense if he is British, or in ignoring the parking regulations if he is a foreigner in London.

The jaundiced ambassador may sometimes be inclined to conclude that he is regarded principally as a service agency: that to the tourist his only serious responsibility is to produce money when a wallet is stolen or to get out of gaol one of his fellow-citizens locked up for smuggling currency or drugs; that to the businessman his sole purpose is to promote the businessman's interests; that to the press correspondent he is there to provide information for the correspondent's copy and a good story out of anything that happens in the embassy; that to visiting politicians he is the provider of free board and lodging and an introduction and shopping service, and that to Mr Le Carré's readers he is the man who keeps the spy out of the cold.

In his more charitable moments he will admit that the tourist in difficulty is entitled to ask for the embassy's help; that the businessman is promoting his country's exports and that it is one of the ambassador's most important duties to help him; that co-operation between the embassy and the press correspondent is useful to both; that he is paid to give hospitality and has the staff to provide services to visiting politicians and will be well advised to do what he can for them; and he will assure you that the only spies whose acquaintance he cultivates are those defeated in the last chapter by James Bond.

Perhaps the ambassador gains some spurious comfort from those writers to whom the diplomat is, by definition, a paragon of all the virtues, brilliantly perceptive, patient, equable, accurate, loyal, modest and of the highest integrity, able to win the confidence of 'the ruling few', handsome, not too witty, an accomplished host, expert in food and wines, widely read in European literature and speaking four or five European languages perfectly (Asian languages do not count towards the score). But he knows in his more sober moments that in real life he is no better nor worse endowed than his contemporaries in other professions, though there is always a danger that the requirements of that voracious god, security, will reduce him to a dead level of unenterprising mediocrity. He knows too that the better informed of the public do not regard him as wallowing in luxury, but sympathise with him for having to keep a government hotel and endure a regular diet of official parties notable only for their tedium and their capacity to induce mental and physical exhaustion.

In the old days the ambassador was purely political. In his heyday he took with him to his post his wife, perhaps his mistress, his butler, his son or his nephew as an attaché and a few footmen and secretaries to round it off. In later times he allowed some inferior life to form part of his entourage, having to do with commercial or consular affairs; but he disdained such menial occupations himself and gladly admitted to a total ignorance of anything to do with the country in which he lived other than the political and amorous intrigues of the court or presidency. Nowadays, whatever his personal predilections, he will recognise that he must give serious attention to matters other than politics. He must regard himself as an economist, a commercial traveller, an advertising agent for his country; he wields the weapon of culture for political ends; he promotes scientific and technical exchanges and administers development aid. He cannot wholly detach himself from the technicalities and personal inconveniences which accompany the battle for intelligence. He must concern himself with the relations not only of governments, but also of politicians, scientists, musicians, dancers, actors, authors, footballers, trade unionists and even women and youth, those two new technical professions in the modern world. But he continues to have a basic political job, to negotiate with the other government and to keep his own government informed about anything in the country to which he is accredited which affects his country's interests.

There are several kinds of diplomatic services within each service. There are the 'grey eminences' in the corridors of power, who shun the light, who learn when to feed those dangerous animals, ministers, pacing up and down their party cages, who acquire an unrivalled knowledge of how government actually works beneath the misleading surface of ministerial responsibility, and who, wrapped in the armour of their anonymity and pricked by secret envy, profess to despise ambassadors as pasteboard figures, strutting their hour upon the stage, but doing no more than speaking the lines put into their mouths by the anonymous script writer at home. There are those few, now very few, who still progress serenely from palace to palace, in peaceful cities whose architecture provides melancholy evidence that power has passed elsewhere, who grow more portly at each translation, living an agreeable civilised life, frequenting the remaining courts, acquiring the noble addition to the chest of the order presented by a gracious sovereign to ambassadors on the royal circuit, if they happen to represent a monarch, but not having to exercise their intellectual capacities to any notable extent, save perhaps in the production of a few elegant translations of Theocritus or a new exegesis of the theories of the Marquis de Sade.

In the British service, there are the addicts of the 'inner circle' as it is called – Washington, Paris, Bonn, with intermediate stops at some lesser stations on the line – who are faced with important and complex problems which are promptly taken out of their hands by eager ministerial and official hands at home. There are the specialists in marxist dialectics, the political cryptographers, poring over their texts, or skating over the thin ice of life in a communist capital. There are those who prefer or have to endure the less fashionable and rougher life in the new centres of power, where they are required to defend their countrymen's interests when the foreigners' property is confiscated by those who consider that they have been exploited in the past and have a right to make up for it by grabbing all they can in the name of the people. For some years during the liquidation of empire, these were the most stimulating posts

for a British ambassador, who had at the same time to play
cat's cradle with nervous and grasping dictators and to try to
convince his masters at home that Queen Victoria was no
longer on the throne and that imperial communications were
no longer a British interest in the absence of an empire at the
other end.

The diplomatic career is not always a smooth progression
from post to post. It is subject to forced interruptions, a kind
of political lock-out, following the breach of diplomatic relations. This growing habit reflects a false doctrine. The
sensible British practice is to establish diplomatic relations with
any government which has control of a country and looks like
keeping it, whether we like the government or not. To be in
relations with a government should not mean that you approve
of it, but only that you have interests in the country which you
want to protect and therefore have to deal with the people who
are governing it. The Americans, less sensibly, are apt to intro-
duce moral criteria and to refuse to regard a government as
worthy of their recognition if they dislike it and hope that it
will go away, though they cannot escape inconsistency when
it does not go away and they have in the end to recognise it,
whether they like it or not. In the meantime their interests
suffer, as they did in China where I had to try to represent
them, while the Chinese refused to recognise my right to do
so, in order to put pressure on the Americans to recognise
them.

The American doctrine has been a bad example, since it has
now been extended by some countries to the breach of relations. This naturally follows a declaration of war or the in-
vasion of someone else's territory without a declaration, like
the British and French landings in Egypt in 1956. But a
number of countries in the Middle East and Africa now break
relations because they belong to a group which wants to show
disapproval of another country's policy on a particular question

17

such as German reparations to Israel or British failure to suppress Mr Smith by force.

This entails some inconvenience to both sides. So the practice is growing that each party leaves bits of its embassy behind and the day-to-day job goes on under cover of someone else's embassy, which is against the ambassador's interests and faces him with a new hazard in his career. Like an orchestra dispensing with the conductor for a familiar programme, it suggests that for most purposes the embassy can do without him. He may find himself forced to leave his post for a wholly irrelevant reason. Governments find it much harder to restore than to break relations, since prestige is involved if one government proposes restoration and the other refuses it, and the home landscape may be dotted for months with fractious ambassadors demanding a new job. I was in that position myself, having been faced after the breach of our relations with Egypt with the cheerless news that six months earlier I could have had any job, but that the vacancies had recently all been filled. After eight months' idleness I received a letter from a clerk in the establishment department that if I did not get a job in the next month, I should no longer be paid. This was the lowest point in my diplomatic career. I reacted sharply and received an apology, but still had to wait for the job.

In the old days many members of the British service used to take a year or so off *en disponibilité*, without pay, but nowadays this rarely happens, since the character of the service has changed and few of its members can afford that luxury. Instead, the periodical bouts of frustration which afflict diplomats in their middle years, are treated by a year spent on the communal therapeutic exercises at the Royal College of Defence Studies or in solitary academic study at Oxford or Harvard, in the hope that the subjects will regain their equanimity and the intellectual habits of their youth. It is however something of a shock for a civil servant suddenly to find himself deprived of the flow of paper which normally channels his thoughts. One such was so unhappy at the prospect that his wife found it advisable to buy him two trays marked 'in' and 'out', which effectively restored his composure.

The diplomatic 'career' is an important trade union in the countries which had old and well-seasoned diplomatic services. The aim of the 'career' is to occupy all the places on the board. In some countries embassies are used as political waste-paper-baskets for politicians whom their president or prime minister wants to move out of the way, or as rewards for faithful supporters of the party which won the last election or revolution. This is fortunately not common in British practice. The British 'career' has possession of almost the whole British board. Only a few strange pieces wander onto it. Some observers hold that this phenomenon is due to the desire of the prime minister to show that he is not in the hands of the foreign office and, if the appointment is from the opposition, that it is made as a demonstration that he is above political patronage. However, the outsiders appointed to posts in the British service in recent years have been highly competent people who have been accepted by the 'career' on their merits and, whatever the purpose of their appointment, have quickly become indistinguishable from the other members of the service.

The Americans generally give the plushier posts as a reward for past political services. At least in the more important posts, they are nearly all men of ability who have made a success of their own career and have the advantage of the influence at home which comes from being in the political in-group in Washington and perhaps sometimes from the party's expectation that there will be another contribution at the next election. The American ambassador at one of the less agreeable West African posts was manoeuvred into it by a persuasive president on the ground that while he could choose any post he liked, this was a really important place for which an exceptionally good man was required, but successful Americans with diplomatic ambitions are not normally naïve and avoid the jungle and the more prickly situations from which they are not likely to acquire any credit. The American embassy in Moscow is nowadays usually held by a professional.

In the old days some very odd fish found their way into American embassies. An ambassador from the American foreign service told me that when he was a young secretary in Budapest, his ambassador lived in a room rented from the telephone girl at the embassy and entertained in my informant's flat. That could not happen now that American embassies are highly efficient products run on standard lines. Moreover, unwillingness to spend money is not an American failing and the extra-mural ambassadors can rarely be faulted in the food and wines which they dispense to the natives on a generous scale. Surprisingly enough, considering the number of American ambassadors from outside the 'career', the American foreign service officers are of a high standard and do not appear to envy those professionals in other countries' services for whom nearly all the top posts are reserved. The American service was decimated by McCarthy and his hatchet boys; but fortunately that form of madness was an isolated phenomenon and is not likely to be repeated.

Monsieur François-Poncet once remarked to Sir Ivone Kirkpatrick and me that the British foreign office was wonderfully organised. The Quai d'Orsay, on the other hand, was chaotic. We rightly suspected that there would be a sting in the tail. He continued that for this reason it was possible for a member of the British service of moderate attainments to become a successful ambassador, while to be a successful French ambassador a superb intelligence was required. I naturally do not subscribe to this theory. It is however generally acknowledged that a high proportion of French diplomats are well furnished with brains and highly professional, their arrogance according to Lord Gladwyn speaking in the House of Lords, being more than compensated for by their efficiency. In spite of their professionalism, French civil servants have their human failings. I have known two *inspecteurs des finances* in the French high commission in Germany, who regularly did their home-work during their meetings with their American and British colleagues, resorting on one occasion to blows before they arrived at a national position. During General de Gaulle's later years, French diplomats who received their instructions from the Quai were handicapped, since the Quai often did not know what policy the General was pursuing through his inner circle. The professionals in the British foreign office will tell you that Monsieur de Courcel was able to be a success-ful French ambassador in London because he received his instructions directly from the General.

Soviet ambassadors are also among the most professional, very competent and well-disciplined, though severely restricted in initiative by the Soviet system which keeps its ambassadors tightly on the leash, and hampered by the necessity of apprais-ing the battles of Westminster or the emotions of the Middle East in marxist terms. A good Soviet ambassador can how-ever make a considerable impact in a non-communist country, if he does not overdo his support of the local communists and fellow-travellers. But it is not always the most powerful coun-tries which have the best diplomatic observers. In instinctive and well-informed understanding of a political situation it is difficult to surpass the Yugoslavs; the Canadians will give you a balanced judgement from their mid-Atlantic perspective and the Canadian Robert Ford is reputedly the best observer in his time of the Moscow scene; the Italians can smell the wind in the Middle East; the Australians are becoming expert on their Asian neighbours, though the policy of their government towards China in the early seventies seemed to be based more on the need to reassure their main protectors, the Americans, of their alignment with the unrealistic American China policy that on an objective appraisal of Chinese policy and aims.

Except in the French-speaking countries in Europe, ambassadors from outside the 'career' are not expected to know any language other than their own native tongue and English; but for members of the career some knowledge of French is a useful if not essential qualification outside Europe, for the purpose of conversation with francophone Africans, and with Afghans and Turks of the older generation, and in order to do French colleagues the kindness of fostering their illusion that French is still the proper language of diplomacy. It is now becoming not only smart but virtually obligatory for members of the 'career' to know some Russian in Moscow or Japanese in Tokyo. A knowledge of Arabic or Chinese is crammed by forcible feeding into new members of the British service who are faced on entry with an indigestible language like a plate of porridge presented by nanny at breakfast. A knowledge of Arabic may however lead to expulsion from an Arab country on the ground that it enables the Arabist to intrigue effectively with the president's enemies. Arabists are labelled as dangerous, which should encourage young members of the British service to become one.

Attempts to talk the local language may be received with genuine warmth or amused tolerance. It is prudent to use it in such a way as to imply that you intend a compliment to the superior culture in which you are privileged to participate and that you are well aware that the recipient of your halting effort knows your language better than you know his. You are on fairly safe ground for the first year, since the natives will tolerantly adopt Dr Johnson's attitude to a woman preaching, which, as Macaulay's schoolboy knows, was that 'it is like a dog walking on his hind legs. It is not done well, but you are surprised to find it done at all'. After a year or so, they will expect you to have improved and will be more critical of your grammatical mistakes and pronunciation. A British ambassador who has spent half a lifetime trying to acquire a slight acquaintance with foreign tongues, moving from one to the next every few years, will end by speaking Russian like a Bulgar and French like a Russian, having in the efflux of time discarded the native notes of Stratford atte Bow. It is worth all the effort involved, if only to be able to read the literature of other countries in the original, and because a sincere attempt, however inadequate, to speak the language of the country is almost always appreciated.

An ambassador need no longer be the first cousin of a 'great family' or figure in the Almanac de Gotha, nor even have been to a 'good school' if he is English, though a readiness to point the right kind of gun at the right kind of bird is still useful, if only for the presidential shoots at Rambouillet or as a convenient alibi when he wishes to see something of a country in revolution without arousing the suspicion that he is surreptitiously carrying silver bars to distribute to agents of the opposition. He may be a member of his country's government. In theory, this is all wrong, since the ambassador's proper function is to carry out policy, not to make it. In practice, it makes no difference, since he can only rarely attend cabinet meetings and has no departmental authority at home.

One ambassador may be a twenty-five-year-old activist rewarded for a minor part in the latest coup: another may be a senior member of his service, but have less influence at home than his military attaché. An official of the Egyptian foreign ministry in Nasser's day remarked to a European ambassador in Cairo that judging from his experience in his own ministry, the only important requirement for an agreeable post abroad was that there should be no military attaché on the embassy's staff. A diplomat from one of the more volatile countries may find himself ambassador one day, foreign minister the next and in a month or two, in gaol. Iraqi ambassadors in London have been known to leave their post unfilled when summoned home to be made foreign minister, in order to keep a refuge from the changes and chances of life in Baghdad. An ambassador may be on familiar terms with his prime minister at home, or not even known to him by name. 'He' may be a woman, known as madame ambassador. If so, she may have a husband, who is classified in Danish protocol as a distinguished stranger, and who will be allowed to paint or collect *objets d'art*, but not to show any interest in politics. Or, as has happened, her husband may be ambassador in another country.

An ambassador may be at the end of a long service in the 'career', bracing himself for readjustment to a life of obscurity or counting the days until he can savour the blessings of private life. He may be in the early stages of his official career, expecting to be transferred to a position half way down the list in his ministry at home or in a larger embassy, for nowadays, when tiny bits of land with the population of an English market town are full-fledged members of the United Nations and have all the apparatus of diplomacy, an ambassador accredited to one of them may be only a first secretary at home. Although a senior French or Italian ambassador retires with the personal rank of ambassador, in most services there is no such rank. It is merely an appointment and the ambassador, on leaving his post, reverts to his substantive rank in the service, known by a number.

Wherever he may be, an ambassador must do his utmost to like and take a genuine interest in the country in which he is living and in its people. He will meet no hostility in countries which his own country has dominated or attacked in the past. The British are not disliked in India; nor in Egypt, where they now say that the British were at least gentlemen. The Dutch are still close to the Indonesians; the Vietnamese from Hanoi as well as from Saigon gravitate naturally to Paris. In Ireland there is still the north which revives historical memories, but the Irish know that Ireland and Britain remain indissolubly tied together by geography and economics and that the two people are still close to each other, and foreign diplomats in Dublin are surprised to find that the clubs still call themselves 'Royal'. But no country, particularly in Asia, forgives indifference or neglect. The ambassador of Afghanistan at the United Nations said to me in an aggrieved tone: 'Why do you not pay more attention to us?'

The ambassador may dislike the government, the policy or the system of the country to which the luck of the draw has taken him. The country may have an appalling climate and be without any of what he has been accustomed to consider the basic requirements of a tolerable life. He may secretly long for a suburban golf-course in Surrey, an Irish salmon river, the Vienna opera, the evening walk along the Madras Marina, the night clubs of Rio or Greenwich Village, according to his background or tastes. But if he dislikes or is indifferent to his temporary home and its people, they will know it and he will do no good there. He had better go home.

And so the ambassadors collect at official functions: politicians, journalists, university professors and schoolmasters, communist party 'apparatchiki', young revolutionaries, generals, contributors to party funds, members of the 'career'. They are all in effect civil servants like their colleagues at home and do not suffer a sea change into something rich and strange when they acquire the title of ambassador. They will probably continue to exist in some form or other for a long time yet, since governments become progressively more involved with each other as they interfere more and more in the lives of their citizens and therefore need their agents abroad. But under the impact of the further development of communications, with the emphasis of each country's interests continually changing, with the formation of ever more political and economic asso-

ciations on a world or regional basis, ambassadors will probably be unrecognisable in fifty years' time as anything related to the scene of today, just as the ambassadors of today have little in common with those grand, rare birds of exotic plumage who preened themselves in the palaces of Europe before the cruel wars of the twentieth century which they had so signally failed to prevent.

Two

Scene Changes

The ambassador sits at his desk and looks out of the window. One sees the elegant gardens behind Pauline's palace and wonders what plans are being hatched in the Elysée up the Faubourg St Honoré. Another sees the heaps of snow and, in the background, fur-hatted figures skating on the tennis-court, and wonders what is happening in the Kremlin on the other side of the river Moskva. A third sees the lush greenery of Rock Creek park, but does not wonder what is happening in the White House, since he has at least ten ways of finding out exactly what is happening there, down to television pictures of the President's operation scars. A fourth sees the palm trees waving in the hot African wind and does not wonder what the President is thinking in the new palace over the way, since the new President is probably the last person to be told what is going on and may only wake up to reality when the next junta on the list comes to shoot him. A fifth watches the workmen putting up the barbed wire on the garden wall and wonders how he can get to and from his office in the morning without being kidnapped as a hostage for the latest batch of revolutionaries languishing in the local prison. A sixth sees the television cameras arrive outside the embassy and telephones for the police to protect him from the demonstrators.

He will not have time to look out of the window for very long if he is in an important country in which his government has major interests. On his desk is a sheaf of telegrams containing instructions in the name of his foreign minister, which for all he knows may have been written by the last joined junior secretary at home. He scans with a critical eye the draft reports submitted by the intelligent, rather superior young men in chancery, of whom he is secretly afraid. He is awaited at a staff meeting, generally known to the British as morning prayers, attended by a selection from his political and commercial ministers, the service attachés, the cultural and scientific attachés, the head of chancery, the consul general, the administrative and security officers, and, if his country is that way inclined, the intelligence officer, engaged ostensibly in some other occupation such as chauffeur or second cook. He is due to see the foreign minister later in the morning. He is to give luncheon to a parliamentary delegation and their hosts. In the afternoon two of the less well-informed of his diplomatic colleagues will call on him successively in order to obtain material for despatches designed to impress their minister at home with the depth of their information and the wisdom of their political assessments. In the evening he must attend an official reception and a dinner which, for political or simply human reasons, he cannot dodge and at which he must exercise all his patience and sympathy in order to find some point of contact with a lady with whom he has no conceivable interest in common.

If he represents his country in a state in which it has no important interests and which is not powerful enough to do much harm in the world, he can sit in his study at ease reading the latest newspapers from home, happily conscious that he can be interrupted by only two clerks and a stenographer, the total strength of his embassy, and that no one at home is likely to make him move to his desk by the inopportune use of the telegraph. An Irish ambassador who, after a life-time of labour as a wine merchant in the Place Vendôme, was enjoying a few years of repose in the Iberian peninsula, told me that the ministry in Dublin had once imprudently sent him a cypher telegram. Having decyphered it himself, he wrote to the minister asking him to ensure that they never sent another one. But this life does not suit everyone. The ambassador may be pacing up and down in an agony of frustrated ambition, longing to make his mark in the service, trying hard to think of something important to do, but unhappily aware that no one at home is in the least interested in anything he does or anything he writes.

It is an indisputable fact that an ambassador is not what he was, but Harold Nicolson has rightly discounted the theory that his importance has been greatly reduced by the advent of the telegraph and subsequent developments in modern communications. If in the old days he had the power to commit his government to action likely to lead to war, he was not going to take risks, but was more inclined to temporise and do nothing. If it took a month to get an answer from his government, the government to which he was accredited was normally prepared to wait for it. If he is now liable to receive instructions several times a day a few minutes after they have left the minister's desk, he can give his own views with equal facility and speed and thus influence the decisions of ministers. If he is now liable to receive the visitations of ministers by air at frequent intervals, he has an opportunity to subject them to the local atmosphere and to instil into them some understanding of the realities which are not always discernible in the heady prep school atmosphere of the House of Commons at Westminster or in the delusive mists round the State department's home in Washington's 'Foggy Bottom'.

The ambassador was one of eight or ten. He is now one of a hundred or more, representing populations of anything from a few thousands to hundreds of millions, and the numbers are still growing. Such is the result of the passing of the colonial era, caused by the concentration of world power in the hands of countries which consider that they have no colonies and which have periodically fanned the wind of change to gale force from opposite sides of the compass with the doctrinal bellows of self-determination or anti-colonialism. It is true that these doctrines were only applied to colonies separated from the mother country by water, the others being too accessible to the forces of the motherland to get away; but enough of them became independent to ensure that ambassadors are now to be seen in most capitals round every corner. The scope of the ambassador's responsibilities has not however been proportionately diminished. The changes in the world which have brought about this increase in diplomatic flocks have also enlarged the field of diplomacy and introduced new complications into international relations. With a whole host of newly independent countries, the painful process of negotiation on a basis of equality has replaced the process of colonial administration, which was relatively painless, at least to the colonial power.

In the past, international relations were managed, or more usually mismanaged, by a few pieces on the board, an exclusively European board. Problems could be solved by simple expedients such as dynastic marriages or by a tidy little war which provided the soldier with a welcome change from the parade ground and opportunity for advancement in his profession. Ultimate power has now passed, at least for the time being, to one Euro-Asian country, which uses its geography both ways as politics require, and one trans-Atlantic country still uncertain of its rôle in the world, and a war involving Europe has become too dangerous a game to play. The only kind of war still allowed by the rules of the atomic age, is a local war in a former colonial territory which does not affect the immediate security of the super-powers.

But the issues of diplomacy are of ever greater importance, since a stupid move could destroy us all in a few minutes. Moreover, the super-powers, unable to use their dangerous toys without destroying themselves as well as everyone else, bound at enormous cost to the infinitely frustrating task of maintaining the nuclear balance – a Sisyphean task – in effect provide a nuclear umbrella for the benefit of lesser powers. Under its protection these have some freedom of independent manoeuvre, though recent events have shown that if a country is very accessible to a super-power frightened of infection from its back garden, it will be well advised not to go too far in asserting its independence. In this new, ever more complicated world, there is still a wide scope for diplomacy and a real necessity for diplomats with clarity of vision, a realistic outlook and the courage to tell their masters the truth.

In the course of his career the ambassador finds himself in a variety of situations. Monsieur François-Poncet, drawing on his pre-war experience in Berlin and Rome, writes: 'When one forms a judgement on diplomacy and diplomats, one should never forget that there are two kinds of posts, very dissimilar. One kind are situated in friendly countries. Everything there is easy. Everyone is anxious to facilitate the task of the ambassador and his staff. Life is agreeable and it is possible to achieve success without great effort. The others are in hostile, if not enemy countries. In these conditions, everything conspires to make the accomplishment of the ambassador's mission arduous, bitter, ungrateful. He feels himself surrounded by secrecy and ill-will. He is spied on and watched. He is isolated. The truth is concealed from him. Press campaigns are inspired against him. His questions are answered evasively and every one of his days is thereby poisoned.'*

Monsieur François-Poncet's picture is too black and white. The environment is not a simple contrast between friends and enemies. All is not paradise among friends nor bitterness among enemies. In a friendly country the ambassador may have no successes to achieve. Relations between the two governments may be so close that their problems are solved by direct telephone conversation between ministers, and the ambassador may not know what is happening. A friendly government may pass through a phase of unfriendliness and the ministers at home may blame the ambassador for a deterioration in relations which they have come to regard as easy and cordial. The political leader with whom he has built up a useful personal relationship may be dethroned by violence, democratic process or coup by his colleagues – the method adopted in Moscow and Fleet Street – and it may be difficult for him to re-establish the close personal connections of the past with the new man. These are the most galling situations.

The ambassador in a less friendly country, on the other hand, at least has the advantage that the home ministers do not expect anything agreeable out of it, and so if something happens which suits their interests, the ambassador may get disproportionate credit. There are other compensations for the ambassador in such a country. He has the intellectual pleasure of measuring himself against the other party and at the same time the satisfaction of getting on reasonable terms with them, which he must do if he is to get anywhere, provided that in the process he does not forget to represent his government's point of view.

The simple contrast between friendly and hostile countries

* André François-Poncet, *Au Palais Farnese*.

represents only a corner of the picture. There is an infinite variety of systems of government and human reactions to be caught, bottled and pinned to the board by the discerning ambassador. There are governments to which every one of their citizens seems to be scrupulously loyal from conviction, training or the need for self-preservation, and where hardly a chink can be discerned in the tightly drawn official curtain, and others whose secrets are canvassed in the press and at the cocktail party, where it is difficult to find anyone, including their own servants, who have a good word to say for them. There are governments rooted in the affections of their people, or liable to be overthrown by violence every six months; governments ruled from the throne or from the streets, controlled by a single party or by a shifting kaleidoscope of splinter groups, genuinely seeking the good of their people or intent only on maintaining themselves in power; dictatorships masquerading as democracies or flaunting autocracy, claiming to represent the will of the people or the will of God. Each variety presents a different human problem. Even the corridors of minor power are never dull.

An ambassador may be living in an ancient palace or in a modern villa. He may find that changing political relationships or unexpected developments in the local scene make his chancery or house unfitted for its purpose or deprive him of them. In Rio the British ministry of works built an enormously expensive embassy in Georgian pastiche just in time for the transfer of the capital to Brasilia. In Bonn they built the chancery on the noisiest road in the neighbourhood, allegedly in order that it might fetch a good price for conversion into commercial offices when the capital moved to Berlin. They now have to build another one. In Moscow the British and American embassies were too near the Kremlin for Stalin's liking and received notice to quit. The Americans obligingly moved, since only their chancery was concerned. The British ambassador, whose living quarters were also involved, delayed the move. Stalin died and the embassy was saved for another generation.

In the Baghdad of the Baghdad Pact days the ministry of works were saved from carrying out their plans for a grand new British embassy on the Tigris by the revolution which burnt the old one and in one day reduced British interests and status and therefore the case for rebuilding more than a modest fire-proof villa. The Americans in Baghdad, suffering from the same political misconception that there would be a permanent Iraqi monarchy within the western alliance, built a fine new embassy on the best riverside site near the king's new palace, too near for the peace of mind of presidents of revolutionary régimes perennially nervous of violence from disappointed colleagues and therefore finding it prudent to fence themselves off from anyone other than those who would be killed with them in the course of a successful *coup*. Diplomatic relations between Iraq and the United States were broken for some irrelevant reason and in due course the American embassy with its grand concrete garden apparently designed to attract the heat, was gobbled up by the succeeding third or fourth revolutionary régime. Now, as an Iraqi has described it to me, not even a bird can fly over the president's palace.

In Cairo the excessive size of the chancery built just before the Suez affair showed how wildly mistaken had been the British assessment of the trend of events. The old embassy in Cairo has been through many vicissitudes since the days of former British power. Some of its old glory and convenience has gone. The cooling winds from the north were blocked by a large apartment building on a site which, according to local tradition, the ministry of works had refused to buy for a low price, thus giving rise to the saying that the British embassy in Egypt never did know which way the wind was blowing.

Its frontage on the Nile was cut off by a busy cornice road, on which in the early hours of the morning would be heard the clippety-clop of the country carts bringing the vegetables to market.

In the ambassador's study, Cromer, Allenby and Kitchener used to look down disapprovingly from their frames on the British ambassador, so much less powerful than they had been. After the Suez *débâcle*, it was rumoured that the embassy would be given up as too grand for the new order of things and for a time those old proconsuls were removed to the ministry's picture store in London. But this line of thought was surely a mistake. To dismantle the embassy and move into a villa would have suggested that we were giving up in Egypt. Wiser courses fortunately prevailed; the embassy remains and a later ambassador has asked for the return of the proconsuls who have a right to be there. We should not disavow our history, at least until someone has burnt it.

I can only regret that the old embassies in the 'legation quarter' in Peking were moved by the Chinese to a new site outside the old city, near some new factories. This was to be expected, since to the Chinese the 'legation quarter' was a symbol of the old domination of Peking by the foreigner. The Russians were allowed to build an enormous new embassy in the northern quarter of the old city, which they completed just in time for the total freeze of Sino-Soviet relations. In New Delhi in the months before independence, from within the department of external affairs, I strove to kill the plans for a diplomatic ghetto, on the grounds that it suggested that the Government of India were unable to protect the diplomats if they were scattered throughout the city, and that in any case diplomats dislike being herded together. I failed; the new diplomatic quarter was established, human requirements having given way to the planners' rigid theories of city development. Mr Malcolm MacDonald rightly refused to live in it and the British high commissioner is still elegantly housed some distance away in one of the older houses of the Lutyens-Baker period. The habit of creating diplomatic ghettoes is everywhere deplorable, though in some cities it at least reflects a practical requirement of the host government, being intended to ensure that the local population is isolated from the foreigners, who can be more easily watched if they are all housed together, and to prevent a politically inspired conflagration from spreading to the houses of the natives.

Wherever the ambassador may be, he is living in an international jungle, 'red in tooth and claw', in which the weapons of subversion, revolution, riot, highjacking and assassination, are frequently employed for political ends, and in which the person and property of the diplomat are no longer inviolate. He is not likely to spend his working life in capitals having an equable climate and all the resources of European or American civilisation, unless he has prudently acquired a tendency to stomach ulcers and a neurotic wife and has carefully avoided all knowledge of foreign languages except a smattering of French. He may have to live for years in a small tropical village which has blossomed suddenly into a capital city, where there is no education for his children, or in a city where he is subject to efficient surveillance, the latest eavesdropping devices and continual attempts at penetration of his staff by an active intelligence service. His wife must put up with all the disadvantages of a gypsy life, knowing that all roads do not lead to Rome, but many of them to distant and unattractive lodgings in the jungle or the desert.

Indeed, he is not the same kind of person as he was in the relatively ordered times of Salisbury and Bismarck; he has not the same prestige; he is not nearly so comfortable. If he is British, he has behind him much less power than his predecessors had. The gilt has come off the gingerbread. If he cannot get used to being, in Monsieur François-Poncet's words, 'spied on, isolated, or having the truth concealed from him,' if he minds being always on the opposite side to the angels, called a fascist, communist, imperialist or by any other fashionable term of abuse, if he is unduly upset by the spontaneous demonstrations efficiently organised against his embassy, he had better choose a quieter profession. But with all the uncertainties and risks, the disruption of family life, the frustrations, the boredom of the diplomatic social round, it is still a rewarding life to the man who, to adapt Milton, has no liking for a fugitive and cloistered virtue that never sallies out and sees her adversary, but prefers a life, even if no immortal garland is to be run for, not without dust and heat.

Three

Commonwealth and International

The British foreign and commonwealth offices and their overseas services have at last been amalgamated. This reform was long overdue. Its opponents used to argue that there was a special commonwealth mystique and that it would upset the commonwealth governments if they had to deal with a single British office of external affairs and no longer with their own office. This argument was always debatable, particularly since the commonwealth governments had single departments and services themselves. As time went on, it lost any validity that it had ever had and the change caused hardly a ripple.

In spite of the dreams of the romantic imperialists, the commonwealth never became a constitutional organism, though British politicians used to and still sometimes continue to talk as if it was one. In fact, the commonwealth is a framework for consultation between its independent members whose interests and political systems now widely diverge, but which still find some spiritual comfort and support in belonging to the group and some practical advantages in membership. I am far from decrying the commonwealth, provided we are clear exactly what it is and what it is not in these days. If the other members realise that the British are as independent as they and are prepared to respect British interests in the same way as the British respect theirs, there is a chance that the commonwealth will continue to exist and will still be of use to its members. If not, the British public will waste no tears at its demise. Meanwhile, events in Uganda in the autumn of 1972 are not a good augury for its future.

A member of the old British foreign service may now serve as high commissioner in a commonwealth country. He will find the work little different from running an embassy, though some members of the service suspect that in the old days British diplomatic offices in commonwealth countries were staffed on the principle that the British high commission must be larger than any embassy or other high commission in the same place, in order to show the importance of the commonwealth and British leadership of it. Commonwealth diplomats are attached to the commonwealth secretariat which holds the ring and can count a commonwealth conference a success if it passes off without a major row. In communist countries which seek to change the ideology of the commonwealth's newly independent states, meetings between commonwealth representatives, even though their arguments are presumably recorded by the listening machines, provide a useful demonstration that the old club has life in it yet.

International conferences called for the discussion of specific political questions are not as common as they were before the age of permanent international organisations and air travel, but they have not wholly fallen into disuse. In recent years, for instance, three multilateral and one bilateral conference have discussed the affairs of Indo-China; one marathon conference at last confirmed the neutrality of Austria; a tripartite conference at Tashkent registered the political advance of the Soviet Union in South Asia and the inability of India and Pakistan to stabilise their relations by making peace or war with one another.

These conferences may be divided into three types. One type is conceived, at least by the communists, as an exercise in propaganda and political pressure. Its effect is wholly unfavourable, since it settles nothing and disappoints the exaggerated hopes which are inevitably aroused, that it will bring about a new and more favourable conjuncture in international relations. Another type is harmless, since everyone knows that the participants do not intend to settle their dispute, but consider it prudent to be seen to be negotiating. The third, unfortunately rare, stems from the conclusion by both sides that their interests are no longer served by the continuation of a dispute, and may even end in an agreement to have a cooling-off period which will last until one side or the other thinks it profitable to start quarrelling again.

International conferences are inevitably conducted in the glare of publicity, which does not help serious negotiation, but where a settlement is contemplated and the essential preliminary of a public deadlock has been established, agreement is reached by private meetings between those participants who really matter and the conference is satisfactorily concluded by a public argument about the wording of the communiqué. A senior member of the diplomatic service from the home team is there to keep his minister on the right lines, and if he comes from a western democracy, to carry on when from time to time the exigencies of domestic politics send the minister scurrying home. The ambassador accredited to the other country most involved may be summoned by his minister to be present as a matter of form, but will find himself almost wholly unoccupied and had better provide himself with consolatory literature to relieve the long hours spent in his hotel bedroom.

More and more, as the world changes, the ambassador will find himself working in or near international organisations, debating thorny issues in public without compromising his country more than his masters have already compromised it, or discussing technical questions of complexity such as disarmament, tariffs, whaling, financial claims or the rules governing the rival invasions of space or the bottom of the sea. These organisations, like children, are great fun in the making, but are apt to disappoint later, and close contact with them can be a most frustrating experience, requiring great patience and forbearance.

The ambassador to the United Nations, known as the permanent representative, is in the most important international seat. The weaknesses of the United Nations are obvious to him. It is a contradiction in terms, since its name is treated as singular, while it is in reality exceedingly plural, its members being rarely united on anything of importance, and using it largely to promote sectional interests. Like its unhappy forerunner which dissolved in war, it has suffered from the misconceptions of its most fervent admirers, the international idealists, who believed that the nations would shed their jungle habits once they were admitted to the club and that it would quickly develop into a world government in a serene atmosphere of international accord. They were unreasonably disappointed when the fair mask, which they had imagined, was removed and, like Dorian Gray, they were confronted by the real face of the nations, wrinkled and distorted by all the old passions and quarrels. The founder members had known better and had prudently arranged that it could do nothing harmful to their interests without their consent.

The United Nations cannot be better than its members, and the more there are of them, the more difficult it is to achieve a sensible agreement on anything. Since it is a microcosm of the human race, its members bristle with prejudices overlaid by self-righteousness, particularly in the discussion of colonial affairs, on which they spend much time, heat and emotion with evident enjoyment. Its resolutions, notably those on the Arab-Israeli dispute, are ignored, since it has no machinery for making anyone do what he does not want to do. It will soon be submerged in its own documents, often written in a jargon requiring twice as many words as are necessary to convey the meaning.

As I write, I have received through the post a copy of the 'conclusion of the international symposium on documentation of the United Nations'. This document records only too truly that 'the United Nations is not above criticism in the sphere of documentation' and that the user should be able to select what he needs 'from among the mass of incoherent information which now frightens him and gives him the impression that there are too many documents,' and it ends on a note of despair with the sad conclusion that 'if it were possible to act on even a few of the recommendations of the participants (in the seminar), the documentation costs of administrations would decrease and, in particular, their activity would be more productive through the increased effectiveness of overall documentation,' meaning in plain English that if the United Nations would do only a little of what was necessary to reduce the volume of paper, its component bodies would do better more cheaply. In a subsequent paper issued by the same body it was calculated that at 1968 prices the cost of making a verbatim record in three languages of a speech lasting thirty minutes, apart from editing, distribution and overheads, amounted to $635.

Diplomats on the United Nations circuit have a mixed bag of responsibilities. In the security council they must debate the most serious issues involving danger to the peace and can acquire a high television rating if they slang their opponents hard enough. The council has for many years been in a state of paralysed deadlock. It now faces fresh complications arising from the appearance on the scene of the Chinese communists, who will at least enliven the old stale confrontation by introducing the internecine battles of the communist world. In the committee charged with colonial affairs the diplomats must wrestle with insoluble racial problems, the task being especially difficult for those who, while agreeing that all racial discrimination is hateful, seek to inject some realism into the discussions of the measures necessary to eliminate it and to apply the same standards to all instances of it, whether those responible are black, brown or white. The diplomats who represent one of the old colonial governments which have given independence to all except the poorest and smallest of their colonies who do not want it, must spend many weary hours in this committee listening to the charges against their governments of the newly invented crime of neo-colonialism, exhibited in their reprehensible habit of continuing to give aid to their old colonies.

The diplomats are required also to battle on the economic and social fronts. They struggle to find a way of making technical assistance effective in countries which, not having been British colonies, have not acquired the administration to support it. They seek to enlarge human rights in countries which subscribe to the universal declaration of human rights while systematically ignoring them. They try to strengthen control of the drug trade in countries which pass pious legislation against it and are in it up to the neck. They vainly promote freedom of information in countries which profess it, but which in practice allow expression only of the official line. They may also find themselves taking part in conferences of the United Nations' special agencies, expensive, glossy and in the main beneficent, with widely varying standards of efficiency, which guard their independence from their progenitor by setting up in different European cities, food in Rome, culture in Paris, atomic energy in Vienna, health and labour in Geneva.

Ambassadors are accredited to the secretary-general. Mr Khrushchev was right when he told Mr Hammarskjold that it was dialectically impossible to be secretary-general of the United Nations. It was the day when the first Soviet *sputnik* was over Moscow, Mr Hammarskjold replied that he had been launched with Soviet assistance from Swedish ground and was in orbit, but he did not stay there very long, and when the Russians had decided that he was no longer any good to them, they effectively limited his power of manoeuvre and weakened his position by showing that even if they could not have him removed at once, he was on the way out. He could have confined himself to acting simply as the servant of the security council and the assembly, but chose instead to use his own interpretation of article 99 of the United Nations charter in order to try and make for the secretary-general a position as an independent peace-maker, acting on his own initiative with a small personal secretariat on the thirty-eighth floor of the United Nations building, wholly independent of the enormous machine through which he was supposed to work.

Mahmoud Fawzi, who as Egyptian foreign minister had been so close to Mr Hammarskjold in the days of crisis in the Middle East between 1956 and 1958, said to me long afterwards; 'I always told Dag that his do-it-yourself policy would not succeed.' Mr Hammarskjold had courage and vision, and if he had succeeded, it would have been the first significant step towards world government, but he was bound to fail. The legal basis of his concept was too weak, the vested interests of governments were too strong and, in the absence of agreement between the most powerful states, the United Nations had no reliable backing for its diplomacy. Moreover, even if he had built a more independent position for the secretary-general, no other man acceptable to the great powers would have been able to sustain the rôle. His successor, evidently feeling that Mr Hammarskjold had overreached himself, showed no disposition to continue in the same path and took no risks. We cannot expect any other secretary-general without Mr Hammarskjold's unique qualities to succeed where he failed, whatever the ambitions which he may nourish and the energy which he displays in the golden first months of office.

The United Nations secretariat is manned by its own permanent civil servants, the real United Nations men, supplemented by members of national civil services seconded to it. It is full of able men engaged on often frustrating labour under the instructions of councils prone to impose tasks of no particular value, only a small proportion of the costs of which are to be borne by the governments represented by the majority of their members. Its proper organisation is hampered by the obligation of the secretary-general to employ a reasonable proportion of the citizens of each member state which can afford to spare them, with a fair cross-section of nationalities in the top posts.

It will perhaps be of interest if I tell something of the story of my own stay of ten months in the United Nations secretariat, in order to illustrate the difficulties inherent in an organisation having an important part to play in modern diplomacy, but deriving its authority from governments with sharply conflicting interests and unable to develop an independent personality of its own. Mr Hammarskjold was by all counts a man of outstanding quality. I had both admiration and affection for him, though he was not easy to work for. In 1958 Mr Dobrynin, later Soviet ambassador in Washington, and I were employed in senior posts called 'under secretary for special political affairs', which Mr Hammarskjold described to me as being like the position of ministers without portfolio in the Swedish Government. I do not know what happens in the Swedish Government, but in fact neither of us had anything to do. Mr

Dobrynin suggested to me that we were Mr Hammarskjold's Anglo-Russian front to cover his close collaboration with the two Americans, Mr Bunche and Mr Cordier, the only officials in the secretariat fully in his confidence, who had worked with him since his appointment and shared his ideas and ideals. That may or may not have been in his mind, though if it were, it would have been understandable, given the constrictions inherent in the secretary-general's position, even if I did not relish being used for such a purpose.

In his relations with his secretariat Mr Hammarskjold was in a dilemma. If he had treated it as a foreign minister would treat a national foreign ministry, he would have had no secrets from the world, and his essays in what he called quiet diplomacy would have been impossible. For public reasons he could not employ me on a serious political mission, particularly on Middle Eastern questions which were then the principal danger to the peace, since I was a member of the British foreign service, with recent Middle Eastern service, and not an obvious neutral. The basis for my employment, apart from routine supervision of the departments of human rights and drug control, did not therefore exist.

I tried to be loyal to him, but it became more and more difficult. When I went to New York, I arranged with some difficulty to be put on the distribution list for telegrams, which was highly restricted; but when I returned from Geneva after the American and British landings in the Lebanon and Jordan, I was told through my secretary that in future I should be shown the telegrams by Mr Hammarskjold, which was a polite way of cutting me off the distribution. As time went on, I had to go to the British mission in order to find out what was happening.

Mr Hammarskjold undoubtedly assumed that Mr Dobrynin told the Soviet mission everything of importance that he could learn in the secretariat, and when he was at odds with the

British over their action in the Middle East, he must at least have thought that I would be in an embarrassing position between the two and had better not know more than he was prepared to tell me. I did not act as informant for the British mission, but slipped up on one occasion. One morning I was in Mr Cordier's office when Mr Hammarskjold appeared, in an angry mood, having been told by the Canadian foreign minister that Mr Selwyn Lloyd had been saying in Washington that he would be prepared for the British forces to stay in Jordan indefinitely – which was not in fact true. Mr Hammarskjold was to give a lunch on the next day for Mr Selwyn Lloyd, to which I was invited. I happened to see Sir Pierson Dixon, the British ambassador, before this and warned him that the atmosphere was stormy, since I did not want British relations with Mr Hammarskjold to go sour. Mr Hammarskjold guessed from his conversation with Mr Selwyn Lloyd that I had said something. After lunch he took me off with him and asked me if I had told Sir Pierson. I said yes. He said, 'You shouldn't have', and never referred to the matter again. He could be understanding and tolerant of others' mistakes.

But I never quite knew where I was with him. One day he was upset by Ben Gurion and unwilling to deal with the Israelis. So he asked me to act as his representative in Israeli questions, but a few days later I learnt by chance that Mr Cordier had gone to Israel to negotiate on the critical situation over Mount Scopus, without my being told anything about his visit or the line which he was to take. I faded out of the Israeli picture and nothing more was said to suggest that I was concerned.

I was called back from leave for the special meeting of the assembly during the civil war in the Lebanon, presumably because Mr Selwyn Lloyd was to be there, for I had nothing to do but sit and listen. One curious incident seemed to me at the time to show Mr Hammarskjold's refusal to admit the possibility of any shortcoming in one of his operations. He had sent to the Lebanon his three observers who, their critics alleged, had allowed themselves to be photographed on the Beirut beach in the traditional poses of 'hear no evil, see no evil, speak no evil.' Their reports suggested that they had observed little of the trickery which the British were sure was going on, but Mr Hammarskjold maintained implicit faith in them and their conclusions. I was bidden to his dinner for Mr Selwyn Lloyd. The conversation inevitably turned to the Lebanon. Sir Pierson Dixon remarked that the observers saw so little that he could only judge them to be either stupid or dishonest. I could see Mr Hammarskjold stiffening and making a conscious effort to change the subject. The next morning he called me in and asked me what I thought of this conversation. I said that it was at least better that if the British thought this, he should know it. He retorted that he had never known such a disgraceful scene, but characteristically added, 'except once, with Guy Mollet'.

There were strange contradictions in Mr Hammarskjold's character. He was a man of superb integrity, immensely courageous, deeply religious and with a strong belief in his mission, but was at the same time a delightful and easy companion. When I knew him, he was shrewd and careful in his political judgement, though, as Mr Urquhart has pointed out in his biography*, he became over-confident in his later years. He was subtle to the point of tortuousness, sensitive to atmosphere and with a powerful psychological insight: yet he could be blind to uncomfortable facts and insensitive to the feelings of others. On one occasion he made a senior official wait six months after the expiry of his contract before knowing whether it would be renewed.

Neither Mr Dobrynin nor I enjoyed idleness in the office. He used pressure by the Soviet Government to get himself

* *Hammarskjold*, by Brian Urquhart

transferred to the post of under secretary in charge of the business of the security council, though, as he said, without expecting that he would have any responsibility in that position. When it was clear to me that I was not going to be employed on any conceivable question of importance, I asked Mr Selwyn Lloyd to withdraw me to the British service, which he obligingly did, since, conveniently for me, there had recently been a revolution in Iraq, which required a change of British ambassadors. I made no secret in my conversations with Mr Hammarskjold that I needed some serious work to do, but there was none that he could give me. I think that in the end he realised that the situation could not continue, though he never admitted it to me. I remained on the most friendly personal terms with him and retained all my admiration for his aims and his great qualities. He allowed no hint of disappointment to appear and I possess a silver salver recording my all too brief and wholly insignificant service with the United Nations. Since I left, the senior British official in the secretariat has been peacefully employed managing the establishment. It is better so.

The question arises: is the United Nations worth while? Should we continue to spend substantial sums on an unwieldy apparatus which sometimes seems to do little but churn out vast masses of incomprehensible jargon? Should we still send some of our best diplomats to struggle with its inadequacies, prejudices and frustrations? I have no doubt at all that those who publicly decry the United Nations and suggest that we should have as little as possible to do with it are making a serious error. It is here to stay. If it disappeared, it would be necessary to create a new United Nations, which would assuredly be less palatable than this one. We should note that the Russians treat it seriously and positively. They will not repeat the gross error which they made in absenting themselves at a crucial moment at the beginning of the Korean war. The Chinese communists who benefited from not being recognised as representing China and from thereby escaping responsibility for their actions to the international community, were wise to refuse political concessions to obtain recognition while the United Nations made itself ridiculous by continuing to recognise Chiang Kai-shek; but once the Chinese terms had been met, they decided that the United Nations was a political forum which could not be ignored and that continued absence from it would, on balance, harm their international position.

Whatever the failures and weaknesses of the United Nations, it is wise to send men who understand their business to it and its specialised agencies. It is a power for good or evil in the world. If it can rarely settle political disputes, it can get over a dangerous situation by talking it out until even the protagonists are tired of it and start thinking of something else. It helped to keep the peace for years in the Middle East, Kashmir and Cyprus, which we are apt to forget. In spite of the deficiencies in its organisation, it can help the poorer countries to develop their economies and technical knowledge. It will gradually produce an international conscience in social policy which recalcitrant countries will find it increasingly difficult to ignore. It can take the lead in combating the pollution of our lands and seas. We must not expect it to solve all the great world problems in a few years, and then blame it for failing in its task; but we should count it as worth all the labour and expense poured out on it if it can achieve some improvement in our imperfect world in the course of a hundred years. And meanwhile it is a public platform for all nations and is looked on by the new countries as their protector and support in a world which is apt to put its narrower interests first, as indeed the new countries do themselves.

Apart from the United Nations and its specialised agencies, regional organisations are now a well-established feature of the international landscape. If a European ambassador is not from a neutral country, he may be attached to bodies such as

NATO, the Warsaw Pact, SEATO or CENTO. Ambassadors to NATO are important people, since they are engaged on their countries' basic defence, though General de Gaulle treated NATO like a mistress officially discarded for being too demanding, but still ready to oblige in case of need. NATO suffers at times from the *malaise* which attacks a planning organisation aiming at so deterring the other side that it never has to put its plans into effect, and from the natural feeling of every member that the others are not paying their proper share. It was founded by Stalin, and whenever it was in danger of becoming moribund, the Russians used obligingly to do something which made it nervous and pulled it together again, though they may now be learning that the game is better played another way. NATO observes with some apprehension that the rich uncle across the Atlantic is not so rich as he was nor so willing to foot the bill. On the other side, the Warsaw Pact suffers from the knowledge of its members that it is as much the instrument for the maintenance of the Eastern European political system against the wishes of most East Europeans outside the Soviet Union as it is a means of defence against the unlikely contingency of an attack from the west.

CENTO and SEATO, both conceived as defence organisations, had to shed the illusions with which they were furnished at birth by western misconceptions such as that the Arabs wanted to be a part of the western defence system and that Mr Nehru would rush to enrol under Mr Dulles's banner in South Asia, and, in the course of time, have become channels for economic aid, mainly American, supplemented by a little planning for defence.

African diplomats, meeting in their own Organisation for African Unity, try to settle old tribal disputes taken over by the new African states, but rarely get beyond registering African quarrels. The Arabs, perennially disunited, can happily proclaim Arab unity in the Arab League, since Arabs give more importance to the expression of their aspirations than to the unhappy reality. The violence of Asian enmities precludes an all-Asian political organisation, and neutral Asian diplomats therefore confine their inter-Asian collaboration to the Economic Commission for Asia and the Far East, that oriental offspring of the United Nations, which mirrors all too faithfully the maternal prolixity. The East Europeans engage in a perpetual battle to prevent the Russians from using the east European economic organisation to dominate their economies. The western representatives in their committee responsible for embargoes on trade with the communists try to maintain a reasonable definition of strategic goods, though they are not always above using the restraints of the embargoed list to gain commercial advantages over each other, and the European members, rightly or wrongly, suspect that the restrictions will be rapidly attenuated as soon as the Americans are ready to trade freely with the communist world. The non-aligned, subtly different from the neutrals, occupy themselves happily in their own club in routine condemnation of their old imperial masters, while defending the purity of their doctrine against the Russians' attempt to equate non-alignment with alignment with them. The poorer countries have their own trade union for squeezing as much money as possible out of the rich.

For the British the world of diplomacy has been radically changed by British entry into the European community. Now national interests must be adjusted within the group, before European interests are promoted by it. Economic integration will inevitably be followed in time by financial and political integration. For us it is a major revolution. Whether we like it or not, it is the lesson of history. A new task faces British diplomats, the task of making the greater Europe, for which we shall need the highest qualities of our citizens, ability, industry and wisdom. Much of this work will be the province of specialists outside the profession of diplomacy, which is no longer for diplomats alone. Here I foresee a danger to the profession. Its members must adapt themselves to the new order of things, or they will find themselves engaged in little more than opening doors for the experts and acting as dispensers of Government hospitality abroad.

International life grows ever more complex and demanding. It breeds initials: OECD, UNCTAD, GATT, EFTA, COMECON. The Russians, eager to spread their philosophy round the world and to have a finger in every pie, belong, according to their own calculations, to more than four hundred international organisations and get from them what political advantage they can. The hotels of Geneva and Bangkok, of Addis Ababa, New York and Brussels are full of the new type of international civil servant, discussing matters which the older generation of diplomats would not have recognised as being even remotely connected with their trade.

Four

On the Habits of Governments and Ambassadors

Sir Harold Nicolson quoted Sir Edward Grey as saying that the aim of diplomacy is to enlarge the area of confidence. This should not be interpreted as implying that the ambassador should consider the improvement of relations as of greater importance than the promotion of his country's interests. He is only concerned to improve relations if their improvement serves those interests. It is not a compliment to the ambassador to say that relations have improved while he has been in the post. The improvement can only have arisen from the coincidental convergence of the two countries' interests, though the manner of handling relations by the governments and their ambassadors has its effect for better or worse. It may be the duty of an ambassador to make relations worse, in order to further an interest of his own government which is not the interest of the other. But Sir Edward Grey's view is true in the sense that

55

even if the policies of two governments are opposed, their confidence that they know where they are with each other is the basis of a successful negotiation. I examine here various ways in which that confidence can be achieved or destroyed.

An ambassador is not normally called on to lie abroad for his country, in the old phrase, and the better governments are not unnecessarily tricky or dishonest, even if they bowl a few googlies every now and again. When the British try a trick or two, they are not very good at it, since they do not always recognise that it is unwise to try to outmanoeuvre an opponent on his own ground. They tried it in the negotiations with President Nasser leading to Sudanese independence and were smartly trumped. Nasser had the advantage in trickiness and local knowledge.

Mr Dulles, a man of the highest Christian principles, conducted the foreign relations of the United States in a way which led others to look for the fine print on the back of the contract, as many American diplomats acknowledge. In 1954, before the Geneva conference, he tried to make out that Mr Eden was committed to his proposals on south-east Asian defence, knowing that this was not true. In 1956 he told the Egyptians privately that they should look out for the French, who were trying to settle the Algerian war in Cairo. At the same time, he was ostensibly backing the proposal to form a Suez Canal users' association, with the intention of making it impossible for the British and French to use force and ensuring that the association would be wholly ineffective. It is not surprising that during this lamentable affair, so full of Byzantine complexities and deviousness on all sides, there was no confidence between the Europeans and the Americans. As in other walks of life, it is wise not to try to be too clever. To the ambassador the tricks of governments are sent by Providence to try him, especially when they are the tricks of his own government and do not come off.

Absolute honesty and complete frankness are obviously not always possible in international relations and the truth is seen in different ways by people with different philosophies and outlook. But the more honest and frank a government and its representatives can be in the diplomatic business, the better. In particular, it is better not to be caught out. The Americans had to admit to having lied in the affair of the U2; the Russians were prepared to lie for a temporary advantage over their missiles in Cuba, though it was inevitable that the truth would come out. We may have professional sympathy for an ambassador who is told to say something which he knows strays some distance from the truth and will be recognised as such by the minister to whom he is to say it. Sympathy is even more due if he believes what he is told to say, but finds out later that his government has been deceiving him as well as the other government. He will at least feel rather stupid. There are, of course, certain well-recognised situations, mostly to do with spies, in which the lie conventional is the accepted custom. No one minds that. But even in those situations it is preferable to avoid direct statement, since if an ambassador has been caught out in a flagrant lie, his statements will carry less conviction in the future.

There are recognised techniques of evasion. In 1970 I said to President Nasser that I thought that he had been careful never to tell me a direct lie when I was ambassador in Cairo in 1955-56, but that he had often answered the question that I had not put. He replied: 'Yes, I often did that.' When I suggested to him in 1956 that he was responsible for subversion in Aden and he replied that he had no agents there, I interpreted this as meaning that he operated through the local dissidents. When I protested against his hostile propaganda on the radio and he replied that he did not control the programmes, I took it as meaning that he had told the director of radio to attack the British Government, but did not actually write the programmes himself. These devices did not destroy the possibility of a serious negotiation, because he knew that we would not believe him, but would recognise that he could not admit the charge.

The Russians are masters of their old national habit of avoiding an inconvenient admission by making a statement which is clearly absurd and which you are meant to know is untrue. There is all the difference in the world between these gentlemanly techniques and the way in which Qasim in Iraq deliberately tried to cheat people. He made a proposal to me for staging rights for the RAF, knowing that in two days' time he was going to take action which he would then declare had destroyed the basis of his own proposal. He passed a special message through a local governor to the wife of an Iraqi politician of the old régime under sentence of death that she need have no fear for her husband, but within twenty-four hours had the man shot. These manoeuvres destroyed all confidence; there was no basis even for disagreement with him.

Apart from the lie conventional and the techniques of evasion, there are the statements which, while not strictly true, are recognised moves in the diplomatic game. When Mr Gromyko said that he would not pay a kopeck for international peace-keeping operations, he meant that a Soviet contribution to the United Nations' ailing finances would only be forthcoming if certain political conditions were satisfied. He was establishing a firm negotiating position, though this technique has the disadvantage that if in the end a concession is made, it tends to discourage belief on the next occasion of its use.

The French, in the fourth republic, used to say that the assembly would never approve a proposal, the Americans that congress would not take it. It was a polite way of saying that they did not agree. The British could not use this method of saying no, since everyone knew that parliament was normally under the control of the government's majority. The Russians are in the habit of saying that they cannot remain indifferent to the action of another government. They mean that they dislike it intensely and hope to make the other government nervous, but it normally implies that they cannot think of any way of retaliating effectively. When we used to say that a Soviet action against a British subject would have a most serious effect on Anglo-Soviet relations, we meant that we regarded the Soviet action as outrageous, but that it was what the British public expected from the Soviet Government and would not stop either the British Government or individual British subjects from pursuing their interests in the Soviet Union, which became apparent all too soon.

Protests are not always what they seem. There are three types recognised in diplomatic practice: the genuine, when you want to show that you are angry, the routine, which are conventional ritual and recognised as such, and the exculpatory, when you want to get in first in putting the blame for some incident on the other side, whether it belongs there or not. Counter-protests are the way of returning the service. The last category is the most common and the game invariably ends in a draw.

Statements of protest are not taken at their face value. What counts is the strength of the retaliation, which is calculated in the light of the effect on the offended government's interests. We protested violently when the Soviet Government invaded Czechoslovakia, but only stopped some football matches and a tour of the Red Army choir. The Russians protested equally violently when we expelled 105 Soviet citizens, an unprecedented action. But they confined their retaliation to declaring a few people unwelcome in the Soviet Union, cancelling an invitation to the foreign secretary, extending their ambassador's home leave and stopping Rostropovich's annual visit to the Aldeburgh Festival. More serious retaliation might have endangered Soviet interests in Britain and the prospects of the projected European security conference, which was an important aim of Soviet policy. It is the action, not the statement which counts.

I must confess to having occasionally used a move not in the book by telling the truth, knowing that I would not be believed, an inverted form of deception which it is only fair to use with people engaged in deceiving you; but in normal diplomatic practice, provided a statement is like a well-known opening in chess, even though it is not strictly accurate, no harm is done and confidence is not destroyed. Indeed, diplomatic deviations from the truth are often revealing. Camus put it well: 'One sometimes sees more clearly in the man who lies than in the man who tells the truth. Truth, like the light, blinds. Lying, on the other hand, is a beautiful twilight, which gives to each object its value.'

Communications between governments become fogged by people assuming that other governments work like theirs and that other people think in the same terms as they do. There are many examples of this in the Middle East. I could never persuade Nasser that every remark made by a BBC commentator or a backbencher in parliament was not directly inspired by the prime minister and represented the British Government's policy, the impression being strengthened by Nasser's selective memory. Middle Easterners in my time could not get out of the habit of assuming that the British Government was engaged in perpetual plots, and that well-known characters like me were in the thick of them. They still believed the old Arab saying that if two fish were fighting in the sea, the British were behind it.

When, for instance, we were engaged in perpetual quarrels with Qasim in Iraq, everyone in the Middle East seemed to believe that I gave him instructions before each meeting of his council of ministers, to which I used to reply that if I had done so, I should have given him much better advice. King Feisal of Saudi Arabia was thinking in purely Arab terms when he told people (including Nasser, who told me) that I was a communist who had plotted with the National Liberation Front of South Arabia to depose the South Arabian Sultans. The realm of fantasy takes over easily in the Middle East, so that an Iraqi could seriously suppose that my appointment as ambassador in Moscow soon after I had left Baghdad was clear proof that I had been plotting with the communists in Iraq to keep the Americans out. In the old phrase, repeated to me by Lord Halifax after the Suez affair, the difficulty is to make two watches tick together in different longitudes.

Another cause of misunderstandings is that the 'ruling few' in different countries do not get the same news and that the news on each side suffers its own distortions. Even in countries like Britain and the United States there is some distortion over a period, not, as the communists would say, because they have a capitalist press and the news is twisted to suit the newspaper owners' financial interests, but for a simpler reason, from the selection of what is news value. For instance, we receive an unbalanced impression of the state of public opinion in the Soviet Union because dissent is news and conformity is not, though the ambassador's reports and a competent foreign ministry will correct the focus.

In the communist countries no one looks for news in the newspapers or on the home radio, which are professedly didactic, on the model set by Lenin, and up to a point, therefore, their distortions, though much more flagrant than those of the capitalist newspapers, have less direct effect. But the communist newspapers do their job, which is to condition the minds of their readers. It is true that the Soviet leaders, with whom other governments negotiate, have their own means of acquiring news not available to other Soviet citizens, if the report current in Moscow is correct that they have on their tables every morning a digest of the capitalist press, known as the *White Tass*, prepared for them alone; but it is surely less likely to be an objective survey than to pick out items of news tending to confirm the Soviet view of the world and therefore hardly conducive to helping towards a common appraisal of the facts in negotiations between the Soviet and other governments.

A common impediment to two governments' getting on the same wave-length is the employment of double standards. Sir Ivone Kirkpatrick, when British high commissioner in Germany, told us that Goebbels had complained to him about a report in *The Times*. Sir Ivone had retorted that there were much more damaging reports about Britain every day in *Der Angriff*. Goebbels had replied: 'Yes, of course, in *Der Angriff*, but *The Times*!' In late 1971 in London, just after the 105 Soviet citizens had been expelled, an East European ambassador said to me that it would not have been surprising if the Russians had acted like that, but that it was not the sort of thing the British did. The implication was that it would not have been reprehensible if the Russians had done it, but was reprehensible because the British had done it. President Nasser, who had probably employed double standards in his cradle, at least recognised what he was doing, when he remarked to me in apparent bewilderment: 'But I don't understand. You are acting just like we do.' The refusal of the African representatives in the United Nations to admit that President Amin's expulsion of the Asians from Uganda was an act of racial discrimination is a flagrant example. Perhaps the British are partly responsible for the use of double standards against them, since they make no secret that they still consider themselves superior to foreigners.

In order to be able to negotiate satisfactorily with another government, an ambassador must not forget that he is basically a *botschafter*, a messenger-boy. If he considers that derogatory, he may recall that Hermes, himself high in the Olympian protocol list, was, in the words of the classical dictionary, 'especially employed as messenger by the gods when readiness of speech or prudence was necessary'. The ambassador's usefulness depends on the belief by the other government that he is an *interlocuteur valable*, that what he says accurately represents the views of his government. In 1956 Chou En-lai said to me: 'We consider that you convey the views of the Chinese government accurately to the British Government and the views of the British Government accurately to the Chinese Government.' I took this as a compliment, since this assurance, however pedestrian it may appear, is the basis of sound negotiation.

The ambassador's views are not of interest to the other government. He may think the other government right and his own wrong, but he must use his best efforts to make the case which he believes to be wrong. If he reaches the point at which he can no longer put forward his government's view with adequate conviction, he is useless to both governments. A curious example of what happens when an ambassador's position is not securely founded on his government's confidence occurred in Moscow during the winter and spring of 1960-61. Herr Kroll, the West German ambassador, represented not the views of Herr Schroeder, the foreign minister, and the officials of his ministry, but those of the chancellor, Dr Adenauer. He established a close personal relationship with Mr Khrushchev through his attempts to steer West Germany towards an eastern policy on the lines which have been recently pursued successfully by Herr Brandt. He was in personal correspondence with Dr Adenauer who supported him, but ignored the foreign minister. The battle on foreign policy was fought in Bonn over a period of some months. The old chancellor was still tough, but was beginning to lose his grip. Herr Kroll was overconfident and talked too much to the press. In March 1962 the *Daily Telegraph* described the affair as 'a spectacle almost without precedent in modern diplomacy. A leading ambassador has conducted a barely veiled feud with his foreign ministry and open hostilities with certain newspapers.' The foreign minister took his chance; Dr Adenauer gave way and after a decent interval Herr Kroll retired from the service. His initiative towards a policy which suited the Russians very well was of no use to them. Once he was no longer supported by his government, his own views were irrelevant.

There are more extreme cases of ambassadors losing touch with their government. A Pakistani ambassador, who was politically opposed to his government, once described it to me as a government of concentration camps and the lash. His early disappearance from the scene was not a surprise. Some ambassadors, with or without justification, have earned the reputation of coming to represent the country to which they are accredited rather than their own. This is no new phenomenon. A century and a half ago, Chateaubriand wrote: 'Ambassadors who are left too long at the same court, adopt the manners of the countries in which they are living: happy to live in the midst of honours, no longer seeing things as they are, they are afraid of letting pass in their despatches a truth which could bring about a change in their position.' That may still happen in spite of modern communications.

There is one instance in recent years of a lack of general confidence in the objectivity of an ambassador's outlook having wider international consequences. I recall Sir Girja Shankar Bajpai, when secretary-general of the department of external affairs in Delhi, coming into my room in the spring of 1947 and saying in tones of despair, 'Nehru has just told me that the only Indian ambassadors in whom he has confidence are Radhakrishnan, Krishna Menon and Panikkar.' Nehru kept his confidence in Panikkar. He was Indian ambassador in China at the outbreak of the Korean war, and was widely believed to be as much a spokesman for the Chinese as for India. On 2 October 1950 Chou En-lai conveyed a formal warning to the Americans through Panikkar that if American troops entered North Korea, China would enter the war. A similar warning was conveyed through allied and neutral channels to the American embassies in Moscow, Stockholm, London and New Delhi. Chou En-lai was putting pressure on the Americans not to go beyond the 38th parallel, and for this purpose wanted his warning to have the greatest possible effect. He made two errors. The use of a number of channels to convey the warning gave it the character of a propaganda exercise, and he used Panikkar. The Americans assessed the Chinese warning as bluff, one of the reasons being that in Truman's words 'Panikkar had in the past played the game of the Chinese communists fairly regularly, so that his statement could not be taken as that of an impartial observer'.* If Chou En-lai had used one channel in which the Americans had confidence, he would have been taken more seriously, though whether that would have affected the Americans' decision to go ahead is another matter.

The time may come when an ambassador's conscience or his intelligence makes him feel that he can no longer serve his government, in which case he should resign from the service. A distinguished British civil servant in the Treasury said to me soon after I had returned from Egypt in 1956 that if a civil servant gets to that point, he should not resign on a public issue in a way which might damage his country's interests, but should wait and resign later on personal grounds. That seems to me to be a reasonable guide. I saw no reason to resign after the Suez affair, although as ambassador in Cairo I had been opposed to the British Government's action, on which I had not been consulted. It was properly their decision which I had to accept and I was glad that I had not been told what they were going to do, as that would have put me in a difficult position. Moreover, the ministers had learnt that particular

* Quoted by David Rees, *Korea, the Limited War*, [Macmillan, 1964]

lesson when the action was shown to have failed, and I wanted to go back to Egypt and pick up the bits, though in this I was not successful, since it took too long to restore diplomatic relations.

Instructions from the more sophisticated foreign ministries are not normally stupid, since the ministries are staffed with intelligent people, but politics may lead the ministers astray, and the officials who have not had their own way may want some help from the ambassador in pushing ministers on to the rails again. Although the ambassador has to carry out his instructions, even if he thinks them stupid, there is one move open to him. If there is time, he is entitled to try to get his instructions changed, but credit can be used up quickly and it is wise not to indulge very often in the luxury of pointing out to the ministry at home their obvious stupidities, unless real harm would otherwise be done.

An ambassador has to have a very special position to do what I once heard Sir Ivone Kirkpatrick do. At a meeting of the three western high commissioners in Bonn, the American high commissioner, Mr McCloy, faced with a complete deadlock over the division of occupation costs and the firm refusal of Monsieur François-Poncet to make the slightest concession, asked Sir Ivone whether he had any proposal. Sir Ivone replied that he had just received his instructions and supposed that he must put them to the meeting, but that they were so stupid that his colleagues would reject them at once, which they duly did. An obtuse representative from the war office, who had come to Germany to make sure that I did not give away too much of the undivided treasure, nearly had a stroke, while I tried to explain to him that Sir Ivone had been negotiating with his French and American colleagues continually for months and knew how to handle them. In the outcome we secured so much money for the war office that even that open-handed organisation could not spend it all. Our experience in

Germany was that the home civil servants were full of fire
in the security of their attics in Whitehall, but that they collap-
sed quickly when faced with the realities of negotiation over
the table, and on this occasion the war office man spent the
rest of his stay in Germany, when not snoring aloud in the
meetings, in breathing down Sir Ivone's neck, urging him to
give way.

We cannot all rise to these unassailable heights, but most
ministers prefer their ambassadors to be astringent rather than
spongy. Ambassadors will do themselves no harm if they fight
back a bit, provided they have sense on their side. In posts
outside the main stream of affairs, the ambassador may be able
to manoeuvre himself into the position of being able virtually
to write his own instructions, but this desirable position can
only be achieved if he has a very close understanding with the
department at home dealing with his affairs.

On the other side, a minister must support his civil servants
at home and abroad. He must take responsibility for his own
decisions and his own words, and should not blame the permanent officials when things go wrong. Mr Harold Wilson
breached this custom, which is an essential part of the British
system, when he wrote in his memoirs, while still holding the
political office of leader of the opposition, that the reason why
he had made his statement that India had been responsible for
an act of aggression against Pakistan was that he had been
'taken for a ride by the pro-Pakistani faction in the commonwealth relations office', I am told that this exculpation did not
impress the Indians, who were brought up in our ways.

A minister on a visit must be careful to keep up the ambassador's prestige and should neither ignore him nor treat him
as an inferior, a mere official. If he does not take the ambassador
with him on his official calls, he gives the impression that the
ambassador is of no account in the eyes of his government. I
have not suffered from this: other British ambassadors have.

Having criticised Mr Harold Wilson, I should record that he took especial pains to support the position of the ambassador when he visited Moscow as leader of the opposition. However successful Dr Kissinger's instant diplomacy in Moscow, it will not be to American advantage in the long run to depreciate the rôle of their embassy which seems to have been kept well out of the inner American-Soviet circle.

If a government chooses for its own purposes to publish an account of an ambassador's confidential conversation with a minister, the minister, if he has not published it first, will be entitled to make the conventional response that he was incorrectly reported and the ambassador's position will inevitably be affected. He can only hope that with time and persistence he will be able to recover it. In 1955 President Nasser told me in confidence that he had bought arms from the communists. However much we disliked it, he had a perfect right to do this and was not contravening any agreement with the British Government. The next morning, the foreign office's spokesman gave the press the substance of the conversation. President Nasser was then entitled to conclude that he could not tell me anything in confidence. British ministers would have been better employed in agreeing with the Americans how the situation should be handled when Nasser should choose to reveal his action himself. Instead, they and the Americans generated much emotion over something about which they could do nothing whatsoever.

And so I come back to Sir Edward Grey's statement. Each party to a negotiation needs to be confident that he can interpret what the other man means, even if he does not say it or says something different, and to understand the background of his thought. And since the ambassador is normally required to represent his government, it should be clear that he has the confidence of his ministers and is accurately representing their views, and that they will respect the confidential nature of the discussion. But the diplomatic course bristles with obstacles. Every diplomat knows that the ladders are few and that it is only too likely that he will land on a snake and have to go back to the beginning again.

Five

On Negotiating

Although a minister or a team of experts can nowadays travel in a few hours to any capital in the world, I hold the view, as might be expected, that the ambassador should always conduct the negotiations with the government to which he is accredited, unless there is a good reason for someone else to take charge of them. A minister of foreign affairs should allow his diplomatic dogs to have their share of the barking and should not be under the illusion that negotiations are necessarily more likely to succeed when conducted by him or another minister on the other side. Special envoys should not be sent from home at every crisis. This devalues the ambassador and makes people think that his government has no confidence in him. Moreover, a government risks one of its more prestigious pieces if it sends a cabinet minister in a crisis to argue with a refractory president, who may think it good tactics to refuse to see him. Sending special envoys is a bad American habit, though fortunately for American ambassadors it is recognised to be a by-product of the economics of plenty and of the competition between rival departments in Washington.

If there are good reasons for a minister to conduct a negotiation in another capital, he must be prepared to sit it out and should not appear to be eager to return home with something to say which will do him good in parliament and the party, for this gives the home team a tactical advantage, since they can exercise pressure by refusing to hurry. It is especially important that a minister should not pay a visit to another country primarily for domestic reasons on the pretence of wishing to discuss questions of serious interest to both governments. In my experience, governments are adept at smelling why a minister is visiting them, and particularly dislike a minister playing home politics on their doorstep. When this happens in Moscow, the Russian hosts are apt to greet the guest with a nasty piece in *Pravda*, in order to show that they are not interested.

Even if a negotiation is mainly technical and needs experts to understand it, the experts may want the ambassador to be in charge, especially if political issues are involved. I have once managed to conduct a sterling balance negotiation without ruining British finances, since I had the expert at my elbow. In any case, a member of the embassy should take part, since the home team will need guidance on local conditions and personalities and the embassy will normally be required to follow up the negotiations when the home team has left. Argument breeds argument and negotiation is a permanent process. The degree of ignorance of some departments in Whitehall about the setting of their negotiations outside the United Kingdom can provide light relief to a British mission abroad. At the time when Germany was still under allied occupation and there was a British high commissioner with a vast office on the edge of the airport at Wahnerheide, a delegation from the department of inland revenue, intent on negotiating a double taxation agreement with the Germans, arrived without notice, passed from the airport without observing the existence of the high commission and were heard in the streets of Bonn asking the way to the British legation.

Experience of domestic negotiations is not wholly relevant to the international variety. It used to be said of Neville Chamberlain that, being accustomed to industrial negotiations in which both sides wanted to find a settlement (a state of affairs which unhappily is less true today in the United Kingdom) he could not understand that this happens only very rarely in international affairs. Ministers and ambassadors naturally do not object if they are given the credit for an agreement which they have negotiated. However, in most cases, the truth is that, after a period of gestation, the parties have at last independently decided that they had better settle the matter on terms which they know that the other side will accept. The important question is generally the timing, the diagnosis when the dispute is ripe for settlement. The negotiator needs luck to come in at the right moment. If he is not going to get an agreement, he will only lose by making concessions and had better be as obstinate as possible. A reasonable flexibility will only pay if he can guess correctly that a settlement is in the offing. The Russians know this very well.

The ground rules for conducting negotiations are, I suppose, much the same for any negotiation, national or international: inexhaustible patience, controlled indignation when required, but not sarcasm. Mr Bevin used to say that you should always resist the temptation to score points. One of the most accomplished operators whom I have seen at work was Dr Adenauer. I can still see him sitting with an amused smile on his face, in perfect control of himself, during an argument about the German coal selling agency in Essen, a subject which surprisingly aroused violent passions, while Monsieur François-Poncet burst out that he was as untrustworthy as his own coal merchants. Sir Ivone Kirkpatrick taught us in Germany the wisdom of reducing every issue to its simplest terms, though my American colleague used to groan audibly when he started an economic argument by his favourite phrase, 'take five apples', and proceeded to draw from his arithmetical illustration the most erroneous conclusions. I also learnt, as a member of the economic committee of the allied high commission, that when you fail to reach agreement and refer the matter to the top, the matter is referred back to you without a solution. Hence comes the invariable and wise insistence that a conference at the summit should be carefully prepared. It is more likely not to end in disastrous failure if the officials can forecast its outcome and draft the communiqué before it begins.

The diplomat will study the psychology and tactics of the ministers and officials with whom he is most concerned, and after some time will learn with whom it is profitable to negotiate, though he can only exercise a limited choice in the matter. In Germany we had the choice of dealing on economic matters with either Dr Erhard, the minister, or Dr Westrick, the state secretary. We came to the conclusion that Dr Erhard, while being always friendly, making a note of our points and promising action, probably threw the note into the waste-paper-basket after we had gone, since nothing ever happened. Dr Westrick would say no for months, but if he finally said yes, action followed immediately. So we preferred to negotiate with Dr Westrick. I made one serious error in negotiating with him. One of my duties was to obtain every ounce of steel scrap that I could squeeze out of Germany, even to the extent of fishing up sunk German submarines out of waters within the Russian zone. When I had begun to despair of getting any more, I enlisted the support of a senior member of the American high commission. We saw Dr Westrick together. The American did his best to help me, but chose to make his points by launching a violent personal attack on Dr Westrick. This interview had a disastrous effect. For a year afterwards I never had an interview with Dr Westrick without his making an emotional reference to the incident.

The Germans did not always react in this way. Sir Ivone Kirkpatrick attacked the chancellor vigorously one morning and was nervous how the Germans would respond at the luncheon party which he was giving for them afterwards. Dr Hallstein turned to Lady Kirkpatrick and said: 'This morning your husband was wonderful.' Sir Ivone knew how to attack without leaving hard feelings behind him. We knew exactly where we were with Dr Schaeffer, the finance minister, who always stuck to his financial last. We were negotiating with him in Paris. My French colleague, having chosen to take him and Frau Schaeffer to the *Lido*, waited with some anxiety for the minister's reactions to the nude girls. Herr Schaeffer merely observed: 'I think that France obtains more foreign exchange from these young ladies than Germany from Oberammergau.'

Negotiations between the allies and with the west Germans during the occupation were out of the run of ordinary diplomatic experience, and it may therefore be of interest if I relate some of the unusual problems with which we were concerned in the economic office of which I was in charge.

Negotiations were first between the allies and then between the commission as a whole and the Germans. They were practically continuous and reached such a pitch of intensity during the preparations for the 'contractual agreements' in 1952 that for several months I had to abandon my office in Wahnerheide and take a room in the American office in Bad Godesberg. It was not always easy to reconcile the views of the three allies. The Germans used to compare themselves to a fish in a tank faced by three fishermen. The French fisherman caught the fish on a hook and laughed to see it squirm. The American put his hand into the tank, took out the fish, threw it on the ground, stamped on it, looked at it, put it back in the tank and started feeding it. The British fisherman let the fish swim peacefully without interfering with it, then turned the tap and let the water out. It was not a fair story, but it got the point.

We were engaged for years in what seemed to me to be the peculiarly pointless operation of deconcentrating the German coal, steel and chemical industries. The allies had taken years to argue out the principles. The Americans sought to make the German industry more efficient in order to be able to reduce their aid, and to make the German system conform to American anti-trust principles, although there were many American companies producing far more than the comparable German companies which we were seeking to split up. The French gave the impression that they were mainly concerned to make German industry less efficient in the interests of French competition. The British Labour Government seemed to have reached the curious conclusion that deconcentration would help to prevent another war and that the way to deconcentrate German industry was to nationalise it and thus concentrate it in the hands of the German Government.

When I arrived, we were engaged in the infinitely complicated operation of carrying out the decisions of principle, and even the Germans realised that they could not dodge it, though they fought on detail every inch of the way. My most pointless task, which took me six months, was to make Alfred Krupp sign an undertaking that he would not again make steel, a requirement which arose from the British public's emotional identification of the name Krupp with the weapons which they had had to face, starting with 'Big Bertha' in the first war. Something was achieved with the steel industry, but very little with coal; I. G. Farben, the great chemical company, was split into three with comparatively little trouble, because the Germans had decided that it would be more efficient in three parts, which could make their own cartel agreements, and therefore confined themselves to fighting over the peripheral companies. In the end, the operation on coal and steel was handed over to the European coal and steel community and it would be hard to find many traces of it today in those industries. For me, in spite of all the effort required, it was a fascinating activity, since it brought me into close touch with German industry, and with the trade unions in the negotiations over the peculiarly German institution of co-partnership. I particularly enjoyed my association with Herr Gunther Henle of Klöckner, a keen musician and music publisher, who seemed to bear no malice after being twice excluded from the steel industry, once by the Nazis, since his wife was partly Jewish, and again by the allies.

We were concerned with the organisation of the 'little civil airlift' from Berlin in 1951, which has now been almost forgotten, having been squeezed out of history by its better-known predecessor of 1948-9. The Russians had been insisting on countersigning the documents covering the transport of goods from West Berlin to the western zones. This we regarded as an infringement of the rights of free access to and from Berlin. For a time the air-lift was effective enough, but the freight charges were more expensive than the charges by rail and the firms in West Berlin began therefore after some time to get their documents surreptitiously stamped by the Russians in order to economise on freight. So we decided to stop the air-lift on the ground that we had lost the battle. The Americans came to the same decision on the ground that we had won it. We were responsible too for the last stages of the dismantlement programme, which ended with the transport of a particularly awkward and unwieldy piece of equipment to the docks for transport to Liverpool where I believe it remained on the quay for many months and was never used by British industry. We realised by that time that dismantlement, however distasteful to the Germans, was most beneficial to German industry which was able to re-equip itself with modern machinery financed by generous investment and depreciation allowances.

Our job comprised a mixed variety of economic and financial negotiations which naturally became more difficult as the Germans gained in economic strength and the day approached for the abolition of the zones of occupation and the restoration of sovereignty to the Federal Republic. Towards the end of my time, on French initiative, negotiations began for the formation of a European defence community, which in the event was still-born. I recall my French colleague suddenly realising that the equality of status between France and Germany implicit in the proposals for the community could not be reconciled with the maintenance by the French of their superior status as an occupying power, and protesting that the French were the creators of the European idea and should not suffer for it. Con O'Neill, then the political negotiator for the British high commission, retorted: 'You went to Balliol, Paul, and you should know that plain living goes with high thinking.'

And so, the allied occupation of Germany was terminated with a grand ceremony in Bonn. The Federal Republic became a sovereign European state. With one matter, the temporary adornment of the Bundesrat, only the Germans were concerned. We heard at the time that a tapestry had been borrowed for the purpose from a museum. Fortunately, someone asked a few days before the ceremony what its subject was. It was the Rape of Europa.

In earlier years before entering the British service, I had negotiated with the Americans on behalf of the Government of India. I had there learnt what an immense difference in relations between governments can be made by the personalities of the officials responsible for them. We had first to deal with the late Mr Wallace Murray, whom we found difficult and openly hostile to the British in India. He left and was succeeded by Mr Loy Henderson. The whole situation was transformed by his friendly and helpful approach, and I have never ceased to admire and respect Mr Henderson as one of the ablest members of the American foreign service of his time.

I recall from those days one negotiation which illustrates the difficulties which arise from the two parties' starting from wholly different points of view. Congressman Judson had promoted in Congress a bill for the prohibition of the cultivation of opium except for medicinal and scientific purposes. We were asked by the department of the interior to enact a law on these lines in India, being told that several other countries including Afghanistan and Thailand had agreed to do so. We had, to say the least of it, our own reservations about the effectiveness of the laws passed by some of the countries concerned and argued that the Indian policy, to reduce gradually the consumption of opium by controlling its production and by heavy taxation, would have more practical effect. Neither side gave way. It was the difference between a doubtful declaration of intent, which would look good on paper, and a practical approach.

National methods of negotiation have to be studied. In western Europe ministers and officials bargain over the table, often all night. It is real bargaining and concessions are made in the process by people who have the authority to make them on behalf of their governments. In Moscow there is little delegation of authority and virtually no bargaining over the table; the pace is much slower and negotiating methods are circuitous. Proposals from the western allies are referred to 'the leadership', those figures in the background who are never identified. After some days the reply is formally presented by the official who received the proposal, probably reading from a written memorandum known strangely as an oral communication, but handed to the ambassador to make sure he does not get it wrong, and drafted with a view to immediate publication. The protocol, maintaining a careful difference between an oral communication and an official 'note', is regulated with precision.

The Russians are never afraid of repetition. They will say the same thing over and over again and will sometimes succeed in wearing down their opponents by inducing a feeling of sheer horror at the prospect of having to go through it all once more. They will maintain a firm position without variation for years, then suddenly change to their last position which they had prepared from the outset. If they have decided on a major step requiring international agreement, this can probably be deduced in advance from a change in the propaganda line. The Chinese also play a match without time limit: their opponent must be prepared to continue the argument indefinitely, if necessary into the next century.

The use of the other man's language in a complicated negotiation, however well you know it, can be dangerous, since it gives him an advantage. Interpretation gives you time to think. The interpreter is thinking only of the language. The negotiator is not concentrating on the business with his whole mind if he has to think half the time about the inflexions of irregular verbs or strain himself to catch the meaning of a phrase obscured by dialect, slang, a cleft palate or deliberate impression. Schmidt, Hitler's interpreter, recorded his view that Sir Nevile Henderson was wrong in holding serious discussions with Hitler in German: that may have been professional pride, but it was probably true enough. The vanity of linguistic ability can be an insidious tempter.

Interpretation requires a special sort of mind and training in the technique as well as in the language. Apart from the United Nations corps, the Russians and Chinese are the best trained interpreters and are absolutely reliable. The Americans, being an amalgam of nations, can almost always produce someone with the right linguistic background. During the occupation of Germany, it was said unkindly of the American high commission in Bonn that half its members spoke no German and the other half spoke nothing else. The British are outstanding in Arabic, as a hang-over from the Anglo-Arab romance, now sadly tarnished. I cannot refrain from mentioning the remarkable Italian Arabist, Amadeo Guillet, a man of outstanding personality, who led one of the last cavalry charges in the history of warfare against the British guns at Keren and, after the Italian surrender in Ethiopia, made his way across the Red Sea to live for the rest of the war as the guest of the Imam of the Yemen under the name of Ahmed Abdullah. As Italian minister to the Yemen after the war, he accompanied the Imam on his official visit to Italy. 'And where,' remarked President Gronchi, 'did you learn your Italian?'

French interpreters vary from the brilliant to the comic. A French interpreter in Bonn once translated an official denial of any *arrière pensée* by the statement that his government had no thought in the back of his head, which happened at the moment to be an accurate reflection of the facts. One of the most brilliant French interpreters was Monsieur Kaminker, who was the hero of the best known story about interpretation. It was in the disarmament commission of the United Nations. The hour was late; the delegates were anxious to get home to dinner; Monsieur Kaminker probably had a date. Mr Molotov had, as usual, made a speech lasting about three-quarters of an hour. The delegates resigned themselves to the interpretations which, by application of the security council's practice, followed the speech. When his turn came, Monsieur Kaminker said; 'Monsieur le President, messieurs les delégués, Monsieur Molotov a dit Non.'

I have seen one first-class British interpreter completely floored. He had had a written text of Anthony Eden's speech at the ceremony of signature of the 'contractual agreements' in Bonn. Before beginning, Eden told him that he was going to alter it. If the speech had been extempore, the interpreter would have had no difficulty, but as it was, he had not the faintest idea what Eden had actually said, and made up most of it. Eden did not know what was wrong and no one else seemed to mind.

The memoirs of life-long professional interpreters like Schmidt are of some historical value, since interpreters are accurate machines with good verbal memories and large stocks of notes, without prejudices to distort the record or personal failures to cover up.

An ambassador must sometimes see a minister without anyone else being present, in which case he will make an immediate record after his return to the embassy. Nasser, whose English was nearly perfect and who did not trust his own colleagues, always saw me alone and would not have been half as frank with me if I had had anyone with me. His suspicions would have been immediately aroused. The only time I made notes during an interview with him was when he gave me his reply to the British Government's statement handed to the Egyptian ambassador in London on the day after the Israeli attack on Sinai in November 1956. I explained to him that I was making notes and would read them back to him, since I could not risk making any mistake. He asked me to leave out his statement that the next day the Egyptians would be defending the canal from the British as well as from the Israelis. Perhaps he thought it was unwise to indulge in bravado at that moment, or was not wholly sure of his position, since he told me in recent years that some of his cabinet were in favour of accommodation.

Normally, an ambassador should always have someone with him in a serious conversation of political importance. Save in exceptional circumstances, a habit wholly to be deplored is for ministers to meet 'under four eyes', as the Germans say. This will inevitably lead to misunderstandings and no one will know what was really said. It is as dangerous a practice if the visitor relies on the other minister's interpreter and takes no one to the interview himself. In an argument about the record, it will then be two against one. However, there may be exceptional occasions when the interview is not in the normal run of things and a special personal relationship is to be established. Mr Heath's conversations alone with President Pompidou in 1971 are likely to be regarded as having been a crucial moment in the development of British relations with Europe.

Six

On Reporting

Apart from negotiating, the ambassador's basic task is to
report on the political, economic and social conditions in the
country in which he is living, on the policy of its government
and on his conversations with political leaders, officials and
anyone else who has illuminated the local scene for him. We
need not take too seriously the suggestion which I have seen in
the popular press that an ambassador is not necessary, on the
ground that a good press correspondent can do the job without
him. The correspondent is always pressed for time. He is concerned more with the blaze in the foreground than with the
permanent realities behind it. He must try and draw conclusions, however speculative, secure in the knowledge that what
he writes will be used next day to wrap up the fish, and that he
will have plenty of opportunities to correct his errors. He must
write what makes people buy his newspaper: if he wrote the
kind of report that the ambassador ought to be writing, the
newspaper's circulation would drop at once. The ambassador

is not required to try to beat the agencies or to compete with all the instant news and comment on the press and radio. His telegrams report confidential discussions. His despatches should be the basis of his government's considered judgement of the international scene. His reports will be radically different from reports in the press.

Telegrams of any importance from British posts abroad and not marked for the recipient only are circulated in the Foreign Office and to other departments concerned in Whitehall. It is an essential part of the system that they are not edited or suppressed. Once only have I known this tradition broken. A few days before the Israeli attack on Egypt in 1956 the ambassador in Tel Aviv sent a telegram recording a conversation with Ben Gurion. The last part of Ben Gurion's remarks, which implied contacts with British ministers unknown to the ambassador or the departments at home, was cut out when the telegram was circulated, no one ever knew by whom. Advance copies, which contained the suppressed passage, were in existence and I subsequently saw one, kept as a curiosity of official life by the department which had received it and which had drawn the correct conclusions from it. But during the Suez affair, the customary relations between ministers and all but one or two officials were broken and all the other officials were neither consulted about nor even told what the government was doing.

Despatches of more than local interest from a British ambassador are printed and circulated to other departments and posts abroad. From them an ambassador acquires much of his knowledge of the international scene in general. If the departments in the foreign office disagree with the writer's assessment, they will contest it in a despatch from the foreign secretary. On one occasion this custom was not observed, when the department did not agree with the views expressed by the head of post in three despatches written just before he returned home. The despatches (not mine) were not printed, only copied to a few posts. In my judgement this was an error. The head of the department should have written a reply from the foreign secretary and both the despatches and the reply should have been printed. More recently, the foreign office disagreed with a political assessment from an important post and retorted with, I was told, a blistering despatch in refutation of the ambassador's views. Having seen neither, I offer no judgement between the contending views. Both were printed and circulated in accordance with custom and the controversy was broadcast to members of the service round the world. This was the correct procedure. These minutiae of procedure may seem of little importance. That is a wrong view: it is on them that the foundations of good diplomacy are laid.

In reporting conversations the ambassador must be honest and accurate; that goes without saying. But his aim must be to convey the sense of the interview in terms which will enable ministers at home to understand it properly. Inevitably, therefore, he must exercise some discretion and interpret it without distorting the sense. He has to tune in to the different wavelength at home. A flat account of an interview, not correctly tuned to the home frequency, will produce a false impression. In diplomatic practice the mortal sin is to report what the ambassador thinks his government would like to hear. This is highly dangerous and may bring disaster. Ideological spectacles, of whatever colour, falsify. The tendentious phrase should be banished from the repertory. A report that a minister took a robust attitude usually means only that he agrees with the views of the writer's government; a report that he was intransigent and obstinate, that he disagrees with them.

The use of some diplomacy in dealing with the home government is recommended, particularly when it is in one of the periodical nervous crises which afflict all governments. The ambassador should not pat himself on the back by reporting, 'I stated your views with all the force at my command, and he took my point.' But I remember an occasion when my bare statement that I had carried out my instructions, which I thought was all that was necessary, was interpreted as meaning that I did not like them and had performed my task without appetite or conviction. On another occasion, my comment that the attitude of the Egyptian Government, which at the moment was not greatly loved by my masters, was understandable, received Sir Anthony Eden's red pencil. I should have foreseen that the old French saying would apply, and that my comment would be interpreted as meaning that I excused the Egyptians for their outrageous conduct in not seeing things in the same light as the British Government saw them. The traditional way for the British foreign office to express its approval is to send a telegram with the words, 'You spoke well.' I only remember receiving that accolade once, and then I wondered whether my account of the interview in question had not been too self-congratulatory and prolix. The reporting course is tricky and the hidden rocks are many. The ambassador can only hope that a judicious mixture of honesty and prudence will carry him safely through.

Telegrams should be brief. Ministers at home have too much to read. 'I saw the prime minister yesterday at 4 p.m. in his elegant villa overlooking the bay. After pouring me out a whisky and soda (Black Label, of course,) from a handsome cut-glass decanter, and enquiring in the friendliest manner after the health of my family,' – openings on these lines were at one time not unknown. Mr Bevin is reputed to have addressed the staff at a British embassy with the words, 'I sympathise with you. You have to cypher your ambassador's telegrams; I have to read them.' It is nowadays more fashionable to draft telegrams as if you were going to have to take them to the local post office and pay for them yourself, instead of handing them to an obliging member of the diplomatic wireless service who puts them on a machine which does the cyphering for you. Nor is it necessary for the ambassador to report that he saw a minister for three hours, as if the success of the interview were in proportion to its length.

A despatch should be written in such a way that it will be read by the people whom you want to read it. A learned twenty-page exposition of the land tenures of Ruritania will be read by the junior assistants in the department at home, if they have nothing better to do when it arrives, or have not allowed their initial enthusiasm to be tempered by a prudent use of the office cupboard as a home for unwanted paper. (A member of the British service, now ambassador in an important post, showed early promise after the war when, after his transfer from a post in the foreign office, it was found that he had left a whole cupboard full of papers which he considered were better left alone.) A minister will rarely have time to turn the first page. The ambassador need not wholly suppress the product of a young secretary anxious to gain credit from his painstaking study of local conditions, but may make his masterpiece, the fruit of so many hours of labour, into an annexe to a terse half page forecasting peasant tranquillity or revolt, which is what they want to know at home.

The author of a book on diplomacy written over a hundred years ago judged that 'fine writing is a most contemptible mistake in an official document'. Lord Halifax rightly laid down in a famous 'minute' that despatches should be written in plain English, not in imitation of the style of Gibbon. It is better to use a flat style than to overwrite, since it helps to make the assessment objective and the style does not run away with the facts. If your fairy godmother bestowed on you the gift of the comic muse, you may give it an occasional airing at the expense of some potentate or bureaucrat requiring defla-tion, or to record for an appreciative but limited audience the utter confusion at the opening of the presidential palace. But be warned. If you overdo it, you will be read, but you will be labelled and will be in danger of never being taken seriously.

An analysis of the policy of another government must be made in the light of its interests, the internal and external pressures to which it is subject, its political doctrine and methods of operation and the whole complex of the national outlook and characteristics. It is a sensible rule to adopt the most simple explanation of a government's action, unless there is a compelling reason against this. Some political observers are too prone to assume that a diplomatic initiative is caused by a desire to divert attention from political troubles at home or by the exigencies of an unconnected situation. It was not, for instance, necessary to assume that the Chinese action in the Taiwan straits in 1955 and 1957 was due to the Chinese government's wish to divert attention from internal difficulties, nor that the Soviet response to Herr Brandt's '*ost politik*' was a concession made in the light of a dangerous situation on the Chinese frontier. In both cases, there were adequate reasons for regarding these actions as conceived to be in the direct interests of the two countries concerned.

Some time after my return from Aden, an Israeli diplomat told me that the Israeli foreign office had calculated in 1967 that Nasser was creating a diversion in the Sinai desert because he knew that I would be manoeuvring against him in South Arabia and that he wanted to divert attention from a situation in which he was bound to be defeated. Stripped of the obvious element of Middle Eastern flattery, this analysis may have been a strain in the thinking of Israeli diplomats at the time. It is true that Nasser knew that his Yemen adventure was failing – it was the one subject on which, in later years, he said he was unwilling to talk – but there were good reasons for holding that his actions in Sinai were based on developments in the area of Arab-Israeli conflict. One must, however, beware of simplifying too much. Decisions of foreign policy are generally the result of a mixture of motives, as in other branches of human action.

In a communist country interpretation of the official texts is the basis of assessment of the current state of relations between governments, parties or individual leaders. In a communiqué after an official visit, 'a frank exchange of views' normally means that there was a terrific row in which the two sides nearly came to blows. 'In the spirit of brotherly solidarity' suggests that one side made it clear to the other that it was becoming too independent for its future comfort. 'An atmosphere of cordiality' may indicate that though one party is on the wrong side of the ideological fence, it is hoped that by the exercise of a little flattery it may be induced to do something to suit the other party's interests. The player of this absorbing political game is engaged in the same kind of textual criticism as the classics don who spends his life happily occupied in the elucidation of a few obscene lines of a minor silver Latin poet.

The raw material of the specialists is not only the official communiqués, but also speeches, articles, the place where they occur in the newspaper, the presence or absence of a party leader at an official function, the people chosen to meet or see off visiting dignitaries, the designations by which the officials are described, the order of the photographs of the top people displayed at national celebrations, the selection, handling and suppression of news and a multitude of clues which, taken together, may throw some light on the darkness which normally covers the struggle for power or shifts in policy in a communist party. It is reported that on the occasion of the celebration of the alliance between Ruritania and Puritania, a senior member of the Ruritanian presidium was not in the official box at the opera. Does this mean that he is on the way out, or has he got a bad cold? The first secretary of the party mentions his discredited predecessor twice in a speech of three hours. Does this mean that the predecessor is to be rehabilitated?

The academic experts at home are apt to think that since they have the same documents to work on and the advantage of many years' back knowledge which is essential in this kind of detective work, it is useless to have the work done again in an embassy by a raw first secretary who has probably spent his last three years in battling with the illogicalities of the Arab world or negotiating with Iceland about fishing rights. But the people in the foreign ministries who receive the embassies' reports know that the man on the spot can contribute something by sniffing the local air, and can sometimes apply a corrective to the experts' conclusions in that other world at home. It does make a difference whether you spend your evenings in a flat in Chelsea or at a 'national day' party at the Praga restaurant in Moscow.

I suggest four among the many points which have to be kept in mind in analysing communist policy. Is a point in an official pronouncement new or has it been said before? This is fundamental and needs specialist knowledge. Sir Thomas Brimelow, who was my 'minister' in the embassy in Moscow, stored facts in his capacious memory like a well-ordered computer, the 'soft ware' being provided by a complete record of Khrushchev's speeches which he had indexed himself. I remember suggesting in 1964 that there was a new point one morning in *Pravda*. 'No,' he replied, 'Khrushchev made the same point in a speech in the Polish embassy in Moscow in November 1956.' Bowled middle stump, I retired to the pavilion.

Secondly – a point well known to all Soviet specialists – there is an unconscious assumption in western Europe and America that stock expressions like coexistence, non-aggression, non-interference and so on, have a universal meaning, while in reality they have many shades of meaning which reflect the political interests or doctrine of the government using them.

Coexistence, for instance, is used by the Russians to mean a struggle for the victory of communism by all means short of war, not 'to live and let live', which is the usual meaning in the west.

The third point is less obvious. I have noted the misunderstandings which can arise from the unconscious assumption that other people's governments work like the government at home. Perhaps we sometimes swing the other way in tending to assume that communist, in particular, Soviet policy is always decided on rational grounds in a rational way. In reality, while the doctrine has a strong influence, Soviet policy is more probably arrived at in much the same way as western governments' policy, as a series of compromises between different pressures and schools of thought, reached after argument and lobbying by special interests such as the armed forces or the KGB, the result not being necessarily based on a cold calculation of the country's real interests. Is it so certain that Soviet policy in the Middle East is based on an objective calculation of the balance of Soviet interests? This is the most difficult area of political analysis, since we simply do not know what is happening behind the façade of Soviet unity, while the Soviet analyst of western policy has the immense advantage that all the pressures on and leaks from a cabinet are canvassed in the press.

Lastly, it is necessary to avoid treating communist policy as if it were carried out not in the real world, but in a vacuum. The effect of Soviet policy in the Middle East, for instance, can only be properly judged in the light of the interaction between the Russians and the wayward, unpredictable Arabs. Perhaps the Russians are now beginning to find this out for themselves.

It is often difficult to judge how far a government believes what it professes to believe about another government's motives. The Russians professed to believe that the expulsion of the 105 Soviet citizens from Britain in 1971 could only be due to a deliberate hardening of the British Government's policy for the purpose of sabotaging the European security conference, a view for which there was no foundation. They naturally could not admit the simple explanation that they had more than their ration of spies in Britain and had refused the foreign secretary's requests to them to reduce the number. The Soviet foreign ministry may have been overruled by the KGB. Their allegation was obviously dictated by the party line, but there was perhaps a lurking suspicion behind it, due to the inherited belief that the British Government, since the fighting in support of the White Russians after the revolution and the Arcos raid, has been temperamentally hostile to the Soviet Union, and the instinct, which may have a grain of truth in it, that, since the British and Russians have certain traits in common, the British are more difficult for the Russians to deal with than the French or even the Americans.

In early 1972 the Chinese were saying that the British, as a matter of habit, leave 'tails' behind them: that, for instance, they deliberately gave independence to India in such a way as to cause future trouble over Kashmir, East and West Pakistan and East and West Punjab. This suited their views in the controversy over the legal status of Taiwan, but was not necessarily only a tactical argument. The vice foreign minister responsible for relations with Britain, who told me this, thought it was Winston Churchill who gave India independence, which, in the light of the Chinese respect for Sir Winston, supports the view that he genuinely believed his theory. If we try to imagine what British policy looks like from the point of view of marxism-leninism to men who have no personal experience of the way in which the British mind works, this seems quite likely.

I have given some examples of the way in which fantasy so easily takes over in the Arab world, converting prosaic British civil servants into Arabian Nights' characters up to the neck in deep-laid plots against true Arabism. Qasim in Iraq was so involved in deceiving everyone else that he almost certainly deceived himself too. I have little doubt that he believed what he announced on the radio, that I had paid £500,000 to the Kurdish rebel leader, Mulla Mustafa Barzani, to raise a revolt against him. How else was the revolt to be explained? Was the action not typical of the British Government and obviously designed to frustrate his just claim to Kuwait? And had he not received a report that I had disappeared up a Kurdish hillside for five hours, obviously to meet Mulla Mustafa, whom I had visited in Baghdad when his party was officially licensed? Was it not indeed quite probable that Nasser really believed, as he said, that the British Government had been responsible for Hussain's dismissal of General Glubb, which he would have judged to be a master-stroke of British policy? My old colleagues would be able to add many examples of curious beliefs, not only from the communist and Arab worlds which I know best.

Whatever the difficulties of analysing policy and opinion in the closed communist world, the ambassador's rôle as a reporter is in some ways more difficult in capitals in which there is a free press, which are the headquarters of a vast international press corps and are inundated with politicians from home, meeting their expenses with a little journalism on the side. Millions of words are poured out on the American scene. What can the ambassador distil out of them which is not already stale news at home? The Monarch visits a neighbouring capital. The ambassador must report the events of the visit with grace, but without flattery, and assess its political results. The Monarch will have the courtesy to read his report, but probably no one else will, for every commentator has wrung the last drop of information out of it. A president is murdered while opening a new gas-works. Millions of viewers see every gory detail on the television screen and every possible political interpretation is exhausted by the commentators who are required to fill a column of their newspapers or fifteen minutes of radio time. And the greatest difficulty of all, whatever the post, is to remember that the local scene, which fills the ambassador's daily thoughts and which seems so important to him, will be of lesser interest to ministers wrestling with intractable problems and trying to keep their heads above water at home.

Let us imagine various ambassadors looking out of their windows at the end of 1972 and reflecting on the people who are the centre of their thoughts. The ambassador is not a professional historian or political scientist. His thoughts are probably neither very profound nor new. But what they want at home is not an academic thesis, but a practical view.

In Moscow the ambassador would perhaps be thinking about the signs of a new consciousness in the Soviet leaders of being a great power with the right and duty to spread their ideas and influence round the world until the sun never sets upon their treaties of friendship, designed to fill the power vacuum left by the collapse of the old empires. However, he would reflect that the Russians are a cautious and even lethargic people, not naturally aggressive, and that they clearly have no intention of risking a dangerous confrontation with the Americans, if only from their conviction that the generals in the Pentagon are irresponsible and might one day induce the president to let them blow the world up. Meanwhile, they are on the way to stabilising central Europe in their interests, and show that they need an understanding with the Americans on the limitation of nuclear weapons, if only in the light of their perennial problem of allocation of economic resources. Even if they do overinsure on the Chinese frontier, they are not likely to let that situation get out of hand. We should be able to avoid disaster, he might think, but should not expect that the dissident intellectuals or even the more flexible younger generation will be able for a long time ahead to change significantly the character of the régime.

In Peking after President Nixon's visit, the ambassador might reflect that unless you have good evidence to the contrary, it is wise to assume that the Chinese mean what they say. They always said what they meant about Taiwan, and should be taken seriously when they say that they do not want to be a super-power or to acquire a dominant position in the countries in which they aid revolution. Why should they want to join the two super-powers in sharing all their wasteful and frustrating obligations, though they will certainly provide themselves with enough sophisticated nuclear weapons to deter the Russians from attacking them? And have they not before their eyes the unhappy experiences of others, including the Russians, who have sought a special position in the 'third world'? He would also not forget that the Chinese time-scale is different from ours, and that they will not be induced to compromise in their political aims merely in order to make something happen in the same century. In the old Chinese saying, the first hundred years of any new dynasty are the worst.

In Washington, where foreign policy is formed through a game of American football between the White House, the state department, the Pentagon and the CIA, in which the White House is normally the winner, the ambassador might judge that on the whole, through most of 1972, President Nixon and Dr Kissinger had assessed Russian and Chinese reactions correctly, though they had in the process upset the susceptibilities of the Japanese and their South-East Asian friends. The ambassador would probably consider that they had made the best of a bad job out of the war in Vietnam, which they had inherited from their predecessors, whatever he might be thinking of the last-minute massive bombing of North Vietnam when the cease-fire was unexpectedly delayed beyond the date of the Presidential election. He might reflect that the Americans had learnt a great deal by the exercise of power since the days when Mr Dulles regarded neutralism as a dirty word. A European ambassador would not allow his government to forget that the Americans expect the Europeans to pay for a greater share of their own defence, though the Europeans can rely on them to underwrite it, so long as they regard it as essential to American security. The British ambassador would recognise ruefully that the Americans nowadays look on the British like a cosy maiden aunt, whom they enjoy visiting as one of the family, but no longer regard as having a serious influence on international affairs.

In Paris the observer in the British embassy would perhaps reflect that the French have never been easy neighbours and that they negotiate as if they were selling a pound of tea and hoped to make an extra halfpenny on it, but he would have to admire their ability to have things both ways, keeping the United States and NATO at arm's length while relying on them for their defence, and remaining on the 'progressive' side of the fence while selling arms to South Africa. Whatever the cross-currents of his thought about those superb and exasperating people, its main theme would be his recognition of the greatness of France and of its place in the centre of British relations with Europe.

Elsewhere, the ambassador is faced by a wide variety of attitudes which go to make up the political view which he must contemplate; in the Middle East, for instance, by the schizophrenia which makes it natural for the Arabs to be genuinely friendly and plot against you at the same time, in Delhi by the high moral tone derived from Dr Arnold via the Indian Civil Service, which the Indians adopt when pursuing their own interests with vigour and ruthlessness, in Berne by the comforting knowledge that the Swiss can be persuaded to almost any unneutral attitude, provided that they can also be persuaded that it does not compromise their neutrality. I forbear from extending the list.

They look out of their windows in London too, as they pause in scribbling their despatches about the 'sick man of Europe' to listen to the BBC dwelling with masochistic pleasure on every industrial dispute and every failure in British production. Truly, they must think, we are a nation of shopkeepers who display every morning a list of the goods which our customers should not buy. Will they ever understand the contradictions in the British character, the strange belief that foreigners recognise British foreign policy to be conducted strictly under MCC rules, the efforts of so many sincere liberal-minded men to subordinate British interests to worthy causes, the difficulty of finding out what the British are after, since they often do not seem to know themselves? Before writing alarmist despatches, they should reflect on the observation made in 1830 that 'there is generally a false crisis every Easter, in which England is all but lost, but she is found again towards Whitsuntide'.* Some, especially the marxists, are probably getting it wildly wrong.

These are only little flashes of the sort of problems of political and human analysis which the ambassador must try daily to understand. He will obviously make a better job of it if he uses the brains of his staff. The way of doing this, which I have found beneficial, is to run the embassy on the Chinese communist principle of the intra-party struggle, by encouraging the staff to criticise the ambassador's efforts as much as he criticises theirs. 'I have done a new draft,' said Tom Brimelow one day in Moscow, 'but I fear that very little of your draft remains.' I was delighted, since the final product made good sense. Too much wrangling between political cooks must be avoided, but it helps towards intelligent political assessment on the marxist principle of the resolution of contradictions if the ambassador can encourage a running debate between two

* Emily Eden, *The Semi-Attached Couple* (1860—written in 1830).

99

experts, prolific in ideas, tenacious in their views and determined to prove each other on the wrong tack. Those who have served with me in Moscow and Baghdad will recognise the pattern.

However well the ambassador understands the people among whom he is living, he will not always be right in his assessments, especially, as I have found from my own failures, if he has to guess the probable actions of dictators, puffed up by the memory of their own successful revolution and adopting conspiracy as their way of life. He must therefore make sure that his position is well-founded at home. The most elementary requirement of good diplomacy is to know where power lies. The British ambassador knows that his destiny is in the hands not of ministers nor even of the press, but of his 'department' at home, which must be the object of his assiduous attention. He will be well advised always to write to the head of the department on serious matters and to the ministers or more senior officials who proliferate in the corridors of the foreign office, only on purely trivial questions such as ministerial visits or the more flagrant misdemeanours of his staff. In deciding to whom to write he will find by experience that nothing of real importance is classified as more than 'confidential': matters which have to be labelled 'secret' or 'top secret' are intrinsically boring. If he is always writing to the top, the top will send his letters down for a draft reply, and the department, annoyed at being ignored, will probably draft something unpleasant.

When summoned home for consultations, he should first make his obeisance to the mandarin with real power, the head of the department, and should leave his brief-case in the mandarin's office, to show that he knows to whom he belongs. He should pay a deferential visit or two to the 'third room' to exchange gossip with the young men who drape themselves elegantly around it, with the object of making them feel that the 'third room' is a cross between a temple of the Vestal Virgins and the bar at White's, though he realises that very few of them can afford the bar at White's and that they are engaged in a perpetual battle against the noise of the telephones and to obtain a share of the secretaries in the 'pool'. He should, above all, seek to pack the department with his friends. If he achieves this, he need have no thought for the morrow. His peccadilloes will be suppressed before they come to the ears of ministers perennially nervous of the press; his errors of judgement will be forgotten; his unfulfilled prophecies will be lost in the files : all will be given unto him.

Seven

Diverse Occupations

Nowadays, when British power has declined and with it British political responsibilities, commerce has become one of the most fashionable activities of most British embassies. The commercial counsellor, formerly equivalent to the third scullery maid, is now often next to the ambassador in the hierarchy and takes charge of the embassy while he is away. The old complaint that British, unlike other embassies, paid no attention to trade, which was sometimes true, is no longer justified.

An embassy's part in commercial matters has been described as marginal, but essential. It is concerned with the negotiation of agreements with those governments which demand them as a framework for bilateral trade. It protests against discrimination in such matters as export subsidies, import quotas, tariffs or the carriage of goods by sea. In Moscow we spent half our time trying to make the Russians improve our balance of trade with them, though they had the advantage of knowing that we thrive on multilateral trade and that bilateralism even to our own advantage stinks in the British Treasury's nostrils.

The day-to-day job of the commercial staff is to promote trade, not to sell. It is illusory to believe, like some British members of parliament, that an increase in an embassy's commercial staff will automatically produce a comparable increase in British trade, or that if businessmen do not succeed in selling their goods, it must be the embassy's fault. The embassy cannot sell their goods for them, but can help those without local knowledge to get in touch with the right people, stop them making the more elementary mistakes, bring opportunities to their notice if they are not equipped to find them for themselves and comfort them in the bleaker capitals by dosing them with whisky and listening to their stories until they are ready to go to bed. On the ability of the commercial staff in these directions rests in large part the credit of the embassy at home.

It makes no sense to suggest, as some do, that we should have the largest embassies where we have the most trade, since the embassy's part in it depends on the type of country and the way business is done in it. Two hundred million pounds' worth of British goods can be exported to western Europe without the embassies having anything to do with it. But the embassy has a special part to play in the developing countries, in which the business in capital goods comes almost entirely from the government. The commercial staff must woo the official customer, whose fireplace displays a row of American, German, Japanese and British invitations to embassy parties. It cannot be denied that the way to this kind of business is sometimes a little muddy; but the embassies, which take care that their innocence in these matters should be beyond doubt, pick up their skirts to avoid the mud and look carefully in the other direction. Trade no longer follows the flag, but the credit. A contract may be won by a judicious mixture of credit and aid, with perhaps a timely invitation to a minister to a visit on the red carpet. The ambassador can help to influence the government at home to adopt policies and expediencies which will clinch the deal for the man with the right goods at the right price against his competitors supported in this way by their governments.

In the developing countries, an embassy is concerned with the politics and administration of economic aid. Those governments which look on economic aid primarily as a means of acquiring political influence are usually disappointed by the results, since aid is a blunt weapon and can have the effect, as Nasser used to say, of putting the recipient in a stronger position than the donor. On the other side, the 'good' people are also mistaken, who look on aid as pure charity and deplore any regard being paid to the donor's interests, but who are inclined to want to tell the recipient what is good for him, like a mid-Victorian lady distributing beef-tea and flannel petticoats to the villagers.

The right view surely is that aid should be regarded as a branch of foreign policy and should serve the donor's as well as the recipient's interests, provided that the donor recognises that it is one of his important interests that the poorer countries should become richer. Aid should not be used directly for political ends, but should be given in conditions which make political sense. It should be used to help exports, provided that it is at the same time helping the receiving country's economy. Mr Hammarskjold's dream, about which he used to talk to me, that politics could be taken out of aid which would be given only by the United Nations on a multilateral basis, will remain a dream for a long time in this imperfect world.

A proportion of aid is in the form of technical assistance. It should not be forgotten that, in an American phrase used to me in Baghdad, many countries have been 'surveyed to death', and that giving elaborate technical assistance to a country without a reasonable standard of administration is like putting the latest electronic equipment on a ship with a leaky bottom. The cupboards of the Iraqi Government are full of the most admirable plans for economic development of that country so favoured in its natural resources, which are deficient only in the fact that they have never been carried out. Aid should obviously not be given where it will be misused, and it is the business of the embassy to try and ensure tactfully that it is used mainly for its intended purpose, but there is a limit beyond which the donor cannot interfere in the recipient's internal affairs. The donor has to walk a political tightrope. He will inevitably fall off every now and again and must reconcile himself to the apparently incontestable fact that the recipient is always in the right and that the donor's aid is not a generous act which will engender kindly feelings, but an obvious obligation which is never wholly fulfilled. There is no such thing as gratitude between states, and relations between donor and recipient, whether states or individuals, are always difficult. In matters of aid you cannot win.

Pedlars of national cultures are found in embassies which have a culture to export. The Russians know exactly what they are doing. They use their magnificent dancers and musicians to earn foreign exchange, and break their contracts as a way of showing their displeasure at a government's action against their interests. The Americans open splendid libraries which they would be well advised to fill with dummy books, keeping the real books out of sight, since the destruction of American libraries has become one of·the world's most popular sports. They teach Asians and Africans to speak English, but somehow it always turns out to have a British accent. The French propagate their *mission culturelle* as a substitute for power. It is sustained by a large application of funds and the absolute conviction that the language and culture of France are the only civilised language and culture in the world.

British culture is mostly purveyed by the British Council,

which is principally an agency for the teaching of English, for the placing of foreigners in British schools, universities and technical colleges and for supervising the Oxford and Cambridge examinations. After many years of floundering, the Council have at last realised that the right policy is to give people what they want, not what you think they ought to want. The result of the change of policy has been an unqualified success. The popular belief that the British Council is more than marginally concerned with the arts and literature is an illusion. Its members are not, as is sometimes thought, recruited from the ranks of the student protesters. They cut their hair, wear dark suits from Austin Reed and are indistinguishable from the crowd hurrying from Cannon Street to the Bank.

In some communist countries the Council is not allowed to operate on its own, presumably from the wholly unjustified fear that if it were, it would be used as a home for spies. In fact, the Council is very prim in its political morals and would never soil its hands by getting mixed up with anything so low as intelligence. So the embassy has a cultural attaché, who is as careful as the Council to preserve his political innocence and can equally well promote such of his native culture as can squeeze through the net of governments obsessed by the dangers of bourgeois ideology. In most other capitals, the British Council preserves its political virginity from the alleged dangers of association with British embassies, and hopes that everyone else will see how independent it is. In fact, no one believes this and the only result is to deny its members the advantage of importing whisky and motor cars free of duty. However, in some countries, it is advisable to keep the Council's institutes well away from the embassy; otherwise visitors will be kept off by fear of having their names taken by the police. Cultural exchanges within Europe have been taken over by the politicians as part of the process of persuading the British that they belong to Europe. The British Council may be marginally concerned, but is likely to become more and more a form of educational technical aid in developing countries.

In the largest embassies the staff list includes miscellaneous technical attachés. For particular tasks they can be useful. An oil attaché in the United States, for instance, can help the British oil companies to sort out the confusion caused by the United States having no energy policy, the resulting vacuum being administered by four separate departments, while the Justice Department, pushing its anti-trust policy to extremes, could rarely be brought to admit that two oil men should even have lunch together, until the pressures from the producer states forced its most ardent theorists to recognise that this attitude made no sense in the modern world. A scientific attaché is useful in the Soviet Union, not that he can provide any technical information which the Soviet authorities do not officially release; but he can help the flow of publications and arrange those visits of scientists and technicians in which each side tries to get more information than it gives.

A rigorous eye must be kept on attempts by departments at home to post attachés where they are not necessary, for the sake of giving pleasant intervals of service abroad to some of their officials otherwise confined for life to the prison of Whitehall. In Cairo, before the Suez affair, when the British embassy was far too large, there was a representative of the Treasury who exactly 'marked' the commercial minister, imitating his every movement, a labour attaché whose purpose was so obscure that the Egyptians must have been highly suspicious of him, and a dear delightful person, John Hamilton, with long Egyptian experience, but whose many Egyptian friends had been submerged by revolution and who did not himself know why he was still there. I succeeded in removing the first two from Cairo, though they only moved to Beirut: the latter, gallant and helpful to our sticky end, retired gracefully in the wake of the withdrawal. In the economic adviser's office in the British high commission in Germany there was an entire office of industrial experts who, as far as I could judge, were the sole consumers of their doubtless well-informed reports. The inspectors abolished them. Though sacred cows disappear in time, their destruction is never a popular undertaking.

Then there are the defence attachés. What, you may ask, are those soldiers, sailors and airmen doing in an embassy? They appear to have fallen into the wrong pool. They lend colour to the scene when the ambassador presents his credentials and on ceremonial parades, but they live a separate life of their own and the ambassador does not know very much about them. To him they appear to be always busy, a sort of grown-up version of boy scouts tying endless knots and lighting ten fires with one match. They feed on maps and charts and technicalities. In friendly countries they spend their time co-doing, as one might call it – co-operating, co-ordinating, co-habiting with the local armed forces. They inspect training camps and cast a critical eye on manoeuvres; they help the arms-dealers, respectable businessmen in these days, to earn their living; they write their reports in a curious formal style admirably devised to convey the meaning in the heat of battle to the most limited intelligence, and are firmly convinced that all Foreign Office reports are written in the manner of 'on the one hand' and 'on the other' and arrive at no conclusion.

Defence attachés are accomplished chameleons, changing their colour to suit their background. My own memories of them are varied. There was Rajendra Singh of the famous cricketing family of Nawanagar, whose chief task in the Indian Agency General in Washington was to feed American generals on real Indian curry. There was Colonel Fraser in the desert near Cairo, being pulled off his horse when he went too near an Egyptian camp set up as part of the defence against a British attack, and organising our defence and the cooking for a hundred people, when we were shut up in the embassy. There was Colonel Bowden in Baghdad, who had walked through a hostile crowd in revolution to join the embassy staff besieged in the chancery, and who, with enormous enjoyment, used every trick to find out whether Qasim was sending his tanks to Basra to invade Kuwait. In Baghdad there was even an American naval attaché, who seemed to be oddly placed several hundred miles inland in a country with a naval force of only a few gunboats. In Moscow there were the 'bears who look over the mountain to see what they can see', as I have described them elsewhere,* and who, in their capacity as licensed gatherers of intelligence, were hotly pursued round the Soviet Union by the KGB, while I used to wonder whether the gentlemen who pieced together the bits and pieces in Whitehall really learnt something from them or just filed their reports away, and whether the attachés would soon be superseded by all those busy satellites, bustling round the firmament, photographing madly. And there are the attachés (not, of course, British) who are expert at buying information from minor members of other people's services' establishments, an occupation regarded as entirely legitimate by any government which can get something useful out of it. The ambassador is happy to have the defence attachés anywhere and for any purpose, if, as he is assured, it is all for the good of his country's defence. In a communist country he will probably enjoy exercising his wits on the intellectual paper game which ensues when one of them slips up.

The consuls are the bread and butter of the establishment. They are spread round a country wherever a sufficient number of their countrymen are in evidence, in order to deal with practical problems such as rescuing the foolish tourist who has got into trouble and guiding the lost sheep among the business-

* *Worlds Apart* (Macmillan, 1971).

men. They are doing the job for which the embassy principally exists, the protection of their countrymen's interests. It is not always glamorous. Some consulates are like the description of heaven in the hymnals, continuous and unalloyed joy in the company of bands of the faithful, elks, rotarians, friendship societies and so on, comfortable, but hardly exciting. But the consul outside headquarters at least has the blessings of independence, apart from the ambassador's annual visit and an occasional summons to a consular conference.

If they are near the sea in Europe, consuls are nowadays exposed to occupational hazards. Lapped in happy contemplation of the local monuments and picture galleries, with only a drunken sailor or two to keep them from the daily visit to that excellent bistro on the quay, a halcyon life, they are suddenly assailed by a package tour finding that their hotel has nothing visible above the foundations, or complaining that the local bingo rules are unfair, that the fish and chips don't taste like they do at home and that the locals can't understand English; or by a covey of popular journalists who have discovered that a pop singer or a distant relation of royalty has been jailed for 'going on a trip'. If the consul is in an Arab country, he may have his windows broken by students objecting that they have failed in their examinations and that the imperialists must be behind it. If he represents a communist government, he is vulnerable as part of a right-wing establishment which does not understand that the true revolutionary doctrine is now an amalgam of Herbert Marcuse and Chairman Mao. If the consul satisfies the customer, he must expect no praise. That is his business. If he cannot do the impossible at once, he will be attacked in the press for shameful incompetence. Salute the long-suffering consul. One day you will need him.

An ambassador wonders every now and again how much advantage there is to British interests in the expensive apparatus for feeding information about Britain and British policies to foreigners, and whether much of it is really necessary. He has to admit that the communications media, to use the modern jargon, are now an obtrusive part of our life and that ministers and officials have to be in the game. Information, as we know it, was ignored by the classic books on diplomacy. The relations between governments were conducted in the chancelleries or on the battlefield. For the people patriotism was enough. Nowadays, the universal passion to inform the masses has given the diplomats something new to think about. Governments vie with each other in the modern arts of information, misinformation and disinformation, the three graces of this strange new world.

The press is still powerful. The top correspondents are very important people indeed, far more important than ambassadors, treated as equals by politicians. They have the entrée to presidents and prime ministers and share their innermost thoughts. They pronounce weekly *urbi et orbi* upon the state of the world and the politics of the Powers. They are courted by all and are ignored at your peril. They are the high priests of the new religion. But, as a political weapon, the press has been overtaken by radio and television. Every black tent in the Middle Eastern desert echoes with the 'Voice of the Arabs' from Cairo. Arab dictators and high officials of the Soviet Government take their news from the BBC. The tenets of contrasting ideologies fill the air in a hundred languages, free enterprise against socialism, revisionism against dogmatism, chauvinism against social imperialism, new heresies against old orthodoxies.

The immense and frightening power of television is extending its boundaries. Ambassadors in London flood the Foreign Office with protests against the television technique which contrasts the palaces of their rich with the hovels of their poor. American mothers could see their sons being killed in Vietnam in glorious technicolour over the breakfast cereal. Jordanians and Palestinian guerrillas, if they wish, can see the black patch over General Dayan's eye. Soviet Esthonians watch and understand the programmes from equivocal Finland. Soon many countries will be able to beam their television programmes by satellite directly into the homes of the citizens of distant countries, which are not sufficiently rich and competent to jam them. Ministers are continually tempted to take up public positions from which they cannot easily withdraw. The pictorial reporting of conflict, the food which the television cameras find most easy to digest, creates more conflict and hinders its solution. Mass communication is a powerful weapon. No one concerned with foreign affairs can isolate himself from it.

The best way of making an impact on the foreign 'media' is at home, through the ministry's news department. Its spokesman is required, without indiscretion, to explain his government's policy, whether it has one or not, to a critical and highly intelligent assembly of correspondents, well able to detect inconsistencies and evasions and to draw their own conclusions, and impatient with a spokesman who is not familiar with his brief. He will give confidential guidance to the 'trusties', the regular correspondents of the great newspapers or radio networks, who invariably observe that confidence, and will fence with others, who, of their free choice, prefer not to put themselves in a position of trust, but to retain their freedom to pick up what they can and write what they will. The best-equipped and most expensive information services scattered throughout the world have little effect for good or ill compared with that produced by the regular briefing of correspondents in the ministry at home.

The ambassador must play his part in dealing with the communications media. He must pay deferential attention to the great men of the international press who condescend to visit him. He must submit to the barrage of questions with which he is assailed at luncheons given by foreign press associations. He must nurse the resident correspondents from home, keeping a wary eye on the less responsible, dispensing the nearest to real information which he dares give them, taking it lightly if they make a good story out of minor scandals in the embassy or criticise him for holding back information, and being duly grateful for the co-operation of the many who understand his difficulties and try not to add to them. For much of his official life he will have enjoyed the luxury of a private and relatively uninhibited expression of his views through departmental minutes; but, alarming though it is for him, there comes a time when he can no longer escape exposing himself spiritually naked, but, if possible, unashamed, to the various instruments of torture wielded by the gentlemen of the radio and television networks, including the innocent-looking cylinder which picks up his incautious asides at a distance of twenty yards.

He is also required to project a favourable image of his country. Powerful countries fling their money about and governments on the way down in the power league find vicarious compensation for lost power in this generally unprofitable form of exhibitionism. If the ambassador is allowed to confine his activities in this field to promoting the sale of his country's goods, he can probably do a little good, though it is hard to measure; but the traditional ways of spreading information like manure look old-fashioned in these days. Embassies are fed with reams of ministerial statements, feature articles and extracts from the home press, illustrated magazines and ancient documentary films. The speeches will have been picked up by the agencies if they have any interest for other than native readers; most of the rest will find a speedy grave in someone's waste-paper basket. The presentation of coffe-table picture books of the beauties of your country is hardly likely to convince the recipient that your industry is noted for its advanced technique, especially if the photographs concentrate on thatched cottages with no drains rather than nuclear power stations. Their distribution is better left to the tourist agencies.

The British information services ought to be well up-to-date, since they are surveyed in depth every two years, so that there is never time to carry out one set of recommendations before the next survey begins. The most effective British activity in the wide realm of information is the overseas service of the BBC, which is why the Russians dislike it. Ministers who want to make it an organ of official opinion should be told to leave it alone. They would not relish having to take responsibility for everything put out by the producers. The worst you can do with the money provided for information is to spread the jam thinly over everything. The only sensible policy is to pick what pays and, with the cordial co-operation of the treasury, scrap the rest.

The tiresome subject of intelligence is much less interesting than the newspapers make out. Some embassies act on the principle that they have no secrets which can possibly be of interest to any other government, and that they need not therefore have any physical security, except against burglars who are after the silver. A secretary of a European embassy told me that in his previous post his ambassador had been sent a safe with a combination lock, but had found it so difficult to remember the combination that he kept the cyphers in a drawer outside the safe. Others take it more seriously, and there is some danger of the security of papers being treated as of more importance than whether the papers make any sense or not. The 'bugging' technicians exercise vast ingenuity in perfecting their defences and defeating the defences of the other side, but the harvest of intercepted conversations is mostly of no interest whatsoever and there is some advantage to an ambassador in being able to give his views more clearly and forcibly to the other side's machine than he can to his contacts in the local foreign ministry. The personal security in his embassy will be greatly improved if he makes it abundantly clear to secret police who employ the weapon of blackmail that he has not the slightest interest in the morals of his staff, who can indulge in any form of sex that they fancy, for all he cares.

The British public is apt to consider spying by other people on the British as morally reprehensible, but the British Government as guilty of a grave dereliction of duty if it does not spy on everyone else. The spy is a member of a respectable branch of the civil service with an unusually large expense account, but rather limited opportunities for promotion in the later stages of his career. Beautiful girls dressed only in pistols do not wait for him round the world. He is not given large quantities of the taxpayer's money to gamble with at Monte Carlo. He is assisted by young ladies of impeccable morals who have represented Roedean at hockey or the Omsk girls' high school at basket-ball. He has a bourgeois domestic life and goes home every evening to the little woman and the kids by the 6.40 train to Weybridge, the Plymouth roadster to Maryland or the Moskva to the dacha off the Minsk road, where he helps with the washing-up after dinner. His main occupation, the collection of the raw material known as 'intelligence', is not glamorous nor particularly interesting, since the interesting part, deciding what to do with the information when he has procured it, is the business of the bright young men in the foreign office, the state department and the sky-scraper on the Moscow 'Ring', who, according to the spies who are a little jealous, invariably get it wrong.

Most intelligence services penetrate each other, forming a sort of club and occasionally meeting for a pleasant evening and exchange of reminiscences. They have the advantage of being virtually free from the security regulations which plague every other official concerned with foreign relations. They are gradually learning that the information which they obtain is not *ipso facto* more valuable than the same information taken from the columns of the daily press. They employ stringers to get caught and occasionally exchanged; but these are regarded by proper spies as an inferior form of life and are not admitted to the international spy confraternity.

There is another class of amateur spies, not professionals of the establishment but used by them, the nationals of the other side's country, who provide intelligence for money or from the misconception that the grass is greener on the other side of the fence. A communist spy of this species who is in danger of being caught in the west, is spirited away to the communist world. He is there kept in quarantine, but after some time is allowed to meet the others who have passed over, who have little to do in purgatory but play bridge with each other and check translations of the local propaganda, and who never succeed in integrating themselves in the country of their adoption. The Western press still takes an indefatigable interest in their doings, and the third wives of well-known ex-spies living on the other side receive about the same space in the obituary columns of *The Times* as lieutenant-generals or heads of Oxbridge colleges. They are well-off financially, since they get an allowance and furnished flats from their former employers, which may be supplemented by drawing dividends from their investments in their own countries and the proceeds of their memoirs.

We all know that intelligence services also organise political operations. Soviet operations have been fully documented. Allen Dulles has written publicly about the CIA's successful operations in Iran and Venezuela, being mainly concerned to show that the CIA never undertook such operations without sanction from higher authority and did not make foreign policy. The CIA have made mistakes – the Bay of Pigs was an obvious instance – but they have had many successes, particularly in South-East Asia. Their general competence is shown by the portions of the 'Pentagon papers' published in the American press, which suggest to the reader that the CIA understood the situation in Vietnam better than anyone else on the American side.

The Arabs have every reason to be nervous of the Israeli service which is among the most efficient in the world. The Egyptians are not up to that standard. I spoke to Nasser in the year before his death about the unsuccessful plots which he conducted through his military attachés. He replied with a rueful grin: 'I tell my intelligence service that the only revolutions which succeed in the Middle East are those we don't make.' He told me also that he had withdrawn his intelligence service from Libya the day before the revolution and that they were in Sollum on the way back when it happened – which he thought funny. The bumper year for plots in the Middle East was 1958: accusations of attempted assassination by the Egyptians and the Saudis, and of Egyptian, American, British, French and Turkish complicity in revolutionary plots filled the radio and the press. How many of them were true we shall never know, though Nasser's complicity in the revolt in the Lebanon is clear.

This aspect of international relations is not new: the tsars were quite good at it in the old days, but it is now a prominent feature of the landscape. An American author has written that 'in the early 1960s a United States career foreign service ambassador at an important post behind the "iron curtain" gathered his military attachés and other intelligence personnel together and told them frankly, "I hate espionage in all its forms". Many CIA station chiefs can testify to a similar reception and attitude on the part of their diplomatic superiors – an attitude which in itself presents a serious management and control problem.'* The Russian attitude as expressed to me, which I have quoted elsewhere,† is that 'every ambassador must have his spy: what is important is that he should not get a bad one'.

* Paul W. Blackstock, *The Strategy of Subversion.*
† *Worlds Apart* (Macmillan, 1971).

Eight

Official Occasions

The ambassador is paid by his government to entertain those natives who may be useful to its interests, not to give amusing parties for his friends from café society, though it will help him to have the reputation of giving a 'good party'. He will hope to have in his house people prominent in industry, finance, science, the arts and the professions and members of the government and of the opposition, where it is above ground and not engaged in making bombs to kill the president, not forgetting either that his principal business is with the government or that the opposition may be the government next year.

In those countries which find it necessary to control every detail of their citizens' lives, even the most distinguished and least politically minded natives will be unable to come to the embassy except on officially recognised occasions, such as the visit of a delegation from the ambassador's country. The ambassador must therefore use these visits to enlarge the circle of his acquaintances. The drill is standardised. A party of visiting surgeons is due to arrive. The embassy obtains from the ministry acting as host a list of local surgeons whom the ambassador may invite to meet the delegation at lunch. The invitations are sent to the ministry, since the embassy has no private addresses and there are no telephone directories. On the day before the party the private secretary finds out from the ministry who has accepted the invitation. On the morning of the lunch he asks who is actually coming. At lunch time he counts how many have turned up and adjusts the table accordingly.

In these countries it will not help the home government's interests for the ambassador to try and evade the system, but each country differs in the limits of social contact which it is advisable to observe, and the ambassador must judge those limits for himself in the light of the political conditions of the moment, neither being unduly restrictive nor going too far off the beaten track. He may find that members of his staff have rather more freedom of action than he has. When he is most irritated at being unable to meet interesting people freely, he has to remember that he must not compromise them and that he is in the country for his government's business and not for his own pleasure.

He must adapt his social habits to the habits of the country. Russians like a buffet supper at five o'clock when they leave their offices. The members of the foreign ministry who are detailed to go to diplomatic dinners have probably had their supper before they come. South Americans think it bad form to dine before midnight. Arabs like to drink for two hours, then eat a large supper and go straight to bed. In many places, diplomats, like cows, eat standing: invitations to dinner are considered to be invitations to a buffet supper which the guests can attend or not as they like, without giving notice. Informality pays. I have seen an unimaginative German ambassador in Iraq, his wife and his daughter, stand for an hour and a half in a stiff row at the door, waiting for a minister who did not turn up, and then sit down at a formal dinner table with empty places. It is better to use small tables, take the most important guests to sit with the host and hostess and let everyone else sit where they like, husbands and wives together, if they prefer it. In unstable political weather, the barometer should be consulted. In fair weather in Iraq our many Iraqi friends were glad to come to our house, as all Iraqis love a party. When the Ba'athists had tried to shoot the president, the security police became active and everyone went to ground. We then saw no one for months till the thaw set in, when, if we judged the weather correctly, they suddenly turned up again.

In western Europe there are other kinds of difficulties. The modern equivalent of the Duke and Duchess of Guermantes may not now find it odd to be invited to dine at the British embassy in Paris with the President of France and his wife, but if an ambassador in Paris does not have the advantage of a recognised place in the world of privilege or intellect, he will despair of ever penetrating the formidable protective layers of French society, divided into intruder-tight compartments. In London a younger diplomat from a small non-European embassy may see no one outside his embassy other than some of his diplomatic colleagues, some kind neighbours in the suburbs and his bored and unhappy wife. He will long to get back to a capital where the government organises the life of the diplomatic corps and provides an official club for them. The foreign office is doing its best to make life rather more palatable for these fish stranded in strange waters.

On national days the few resident ambassadors used to hold parties for their own communities. Now, in many posts, over a hundred ambassadors will hold a national day party during the year and will invite local ministers and officials and their diplomatic colleagues. Some ambassadors, on the excuse of celebrating the crucial moments of their revolution or their great religious days, will, regrettably, hold two or three. Army days are now in vogue, and if ever there is a day otherwise free of official parties, there is bound to be a visiting dignitary who rates a party by the host government and another by his own ambassador. In all except the larger western capitals, where the ambassador happily need meet only the colleagues whom he likes, he must try and attend all the official parties. If he misses one, especially of a small country, without a plausible excuse, he will cause offence.

These parties can however have their uses, especially in the communist world. The ambassador can calculate from the level of attendance of members of the local party and government where in the game of political snakes and ladders Ruritania stands at the moment. He can get to know men whom he finds it difficult to see in their offices. He can exchange views with his colleagues without the trouble of visiting them. He can analyse the platitudes in the speeches. Only in this spirit can the nightly punishment be borne. This habit of giving parties which it is a duty but no pleasure to attend even flourishes in the United Nations, where there is no excuse whatever for them, since the guests see each other every day in the corridors. But one must take them in a charitable spirit. After all, for the smaller, newer countries, the national day is the great day of the year.

Circular entertainment of and by diplomatic colleagues cannot be avoided in many capitals. It is like painting the Forth Bridge. Once you have finished, it is time to start again. Colleagues newly arrived and colleagues about to leave are given endless dinners of welcome or farewell, accompanied by the same conventional speeches. The sensible diplomat keeps his departure secret until the last possible moment. It is no aspersion on the many friends among our diplomatic colleagues of the past to say that recollection of the diplomatic social round induces a sense of weariness and penance.

The Congress of Vienna codified the nice gradation of

ambassadors, ministers and agents, the extraordinary and pleni-
potentiary at the top and the ordinary and impotent at the
bottom. The last vestiges of these distinctions were obliterated
by the Americans who, wishing to flatter their Central and
South American satellites, raised the status of their legations
throughout the western hemisphere to that of embassies, an
action which naturally caused everyone to follow suit, the last,
with great reluctance, being the Swiss and the Swedes who
traditionally preferred legations.

All heads of fully constituted missions are therefore now
ambassadors, and many of them, for some atavistic reason, enjoy being called Your Excellency. Sir Harold Nicolson rightly
characterised this title as outworn. It is still prudent to use it
when addressing those colleagues who appear to like it. It is
on the way out in Europe, but survives in its pristine strength
in the developing world. It sounds rather better in French
with an overtone of mockery. It is at its most absurd in countries which change their governments every few months, each
member of each government retaining the title of Excellency
for life. Some wives of ambassadors like to be called Her
Excellency. It is better to humour them. It has been known for
an ambassador and his wife to insist that their staff refer to
them collectively as TTEE, which has a veterinary flavour
about it. The title of ambassadress has been recorded as in use
from the sixteenth century, but four hundred years is surely
enough, now that ambassadors' wives grow under every hedge-
row. It is however useful when you cannot remember the
lady's name. The ambassador's house is regrettably coming to
be known as the 'residence', which is all very well in French,
but in English sounds like a house agent's advertisement for
a semi-detached in the suburbs. 'Her Britannic Majesty's
Ambassador' is pompous and should be kept to official documents.

On official occasions the ambassador sits in the official seat in his car. According to protocol he should do so even if he is accompanying his foreign minister, since he represents his head of state, though it is advisable that he should not insist on this, if he wants promotion in the service. A few ambassadors insist on sitting there always, which is silly. It is a help towards the acquisition of the local language to sit as often as possible by the driver. When, as ambassador in Moscow, I was sitting there while taking guests from the airport, I was delighted to be asked by Sir Malcolm Sargent what I did in the embassy, to the unrestrained amusement of the other guest, Lord Boothby. But the driver's feelings have to be considered. In Japan the driver will put some luggage on the front seat to force his passenger into the back, since to be seen with a passenger by his side lowers his prestige in the eyes of his compatriots. I have never been able satisfactorily to ascertain the correct car protocol. Is the official seat always on the right? Or is it behind the flag, as is held by one school of thought? What if there are two flags, as there used to be in Egypt, or if the flag was fixed by the ministry of works on the wrong side? Does it make a difference if the rule of the road is right or left? The matter is left in agreeable obscurity.

Protocol is a useful servant, but should be kept in its place. It has its malicious side. It ensures that the ambassador sits next to the same person at dinner for months on end, and requires the host to put together persons who are unable to communicate with each other or dislike each other intensely. Communist governments keep protocol much more strictly than the capitalists. The ambassador has to watch that it is not being used to make a political point, like the insertion into the receiving line at an official party of the representative of a revolutionary movement which has not acquired diplomatic status, a misuse of diplomatic practice which once in Moscow caused the western ambassadors below the joker in the pack to walk out.

Whether to attend an official party or not is a political decision. Save in exceptional circumstances, an ambassador does not attend when the party is given for a representative of a state with which his government is not in diplomatic relations. The device of sending a junior member of the staff, which the Swiss used to practise in Peking, makes no sense, since in diplomatic terms it is the same as the ambassador's going himself. In many countries the whole diplomatic corps is invited to an official party, including many ambassadors who do not recognise some of the others. They all go; otherwise they would never go anywhere. The tendency is to take a stricter view about private parties. In Moscow before my time the press made a good story out of a private party given by the Burmese ambassador, from which some ambassadors walked out, since the East German representative was one of the guests. My American colleague in Moscow used to take an annual risk by getting off in one party all the ambassadors of countries which the United States recognised and making them draw for dinner partners. Fortunately, when I was there, no Arab ambassador drew the Israeli ambassador's wife.

The pointed absence or walk out on official occasions can be overdone, but is necessary if a speech by the host is directly insulting to the ambassador's country. It does not have the slightest effect on the hosts, who will continue their public insults so long as that is their current political line, but the ambassador knows that the correspondents will make a good story out of it either way and that it will be better for his own image to appear as a stout defender of his country's honour. The normal rule is to pay no attention to generalities about imperialists or other conventional terms of abuse which do not particularise their object, since the speaker would gain a point if you admitted that your country was in one of those categories, but to leave if your government is attacked by name. The Chinese and Russians walk out of each others' parties with unfailing regularity. It is awkward for an ambassador to have to sit through speeches in a language which he does not know perfectly, without having an interpreter at hand. It is a golden rule never to clap what you do not understand, unless you are sure that the speaker is firmly on your side.

Similar principles apply to making protests, one of the ambassador's routine occupations in countries where, for one reason or another, he is on the other side of the fence, but there are exceptions. In Iraq the Arabic press used to pad its columns with accusations of British complicity in all the crimes attributed by Gibbon to Pope John XXII. Even when the attack was specifically directed against the British and not merely against the generalised imperialists, it would have been pointless to make a formal protest, which would have delighted the editors as showing that someone paid attention to their appalling rags. The articles were pure routine and no one paid the slightest attention to these conventional epithets, which from continual repetition had long become completely meaningless. But if members of the embassy were accused, we protested vigorously. That was not a routine matter.

In the old days the British did not condescend to have a protocol department in London, since ambassadors to the Court of St James's knew their way around without one. Now that ambassadors are lower in the social scale, they need help in finding where to hire the butler for the evening and how to get the whisky without paying tax, though the department behaves in a frosty British way if asked for guidance on the procurement of female companions. Some years ago, the British foreign office were moved to sponsor a book on protocol for the benefit of the more inexperienced or rebellious members of the service. It is popularly believed to have been leaked with malicious intent by a member of the British embassy in Washington and was the subject of ironic comment in the American press. Mr Ernest Bevin, then Foreign Secretary, had not been consulted. His private secretary put it into his box one evening in a spirit of genial provocation. Next morning the bell rang furiously. He rounded on his staff: 'Who's this man Cheke? His world's dead. Send a telegram to my stations cancelling it.' It was not in his style.

I read it many years ago. My imperfect memory suggests that it was written like a guide to deportment for young ladies, but I am assured by high authority in the service that it could be classed as literature. It has been superseded. I have not read its successor, being no longer in need of its advice. There were two infallible indications that a junior member of the staff had read it. One was when he came up to you at a party, waited until he could interrupt your conversation, breathlessly interjected 'Good evening, sir,' and bolted for cover. What the point of this manoeuvre was, I have never been able to discover. The other was when a man appointed to your embassy wrote saying that the one ambition of his life had been fulfilled, a very proper sentiment, and added a wish to know if there was any little thing he could do for you in England. One man got landed with transporting fifty potted plants, all of which were destroyed by the Customs on his arrival.

The dean of the diplomatic corps is the ambassador who presented his credentials first. He is captain of the school for a brief period until he leaves and is followed by the next on the diplomatic list. When he is the representative of a country not recognised by all members of the corps, the ambassadors who do not recognise him use the most senior ambassador recognised by both as a go-between. This sounds simple enough, but invariably involves much heart-searching and consultation with governments. In many places the dean is of little practical use to the corps, since his flock are hopelessly divided on any issue affecting the local government. They are however united in maintaining their privileges, especially the duty-free cars and drink, and the effort necessary to resist encroachments on them produces a solidarity transcending the most diverse political opinions.

By long established practice every new ambassador is supposed to call on all the rest; wives likewise. Traditionally, the calls are returned. Attempts to abolish this time-consuming practice meet with strong opposition, since the ambassador of a country which keeps diplomats for show rather than use, would otherwise have nothing to do. The calls are perhaps only completed half way down the list, when the ambassador is moved and his successor starts them all over again. Return calls are now being discarded in the larger capitals, but the custom is only being pared away at the edges and dies hard. It is particularly pointless in large capitals where there is a flood of information available. In communist countries ambassadors are thrown on each others' company and have to spend much time exchanging the snippets of information which are all that percolates through the official security screen. Many lasting friendships are formed in these conditions.

Communist leaders, who manage not only the government, but the industry, agriculture and the whole life of the country, organise their day so efficiently that they always have plenty of time for visitors. Their most time-consuming custom is the ceremony of the airport. The arrival and departure of each visitor of a certain rank or of the local top brass, requires the presence of appropriate members of the party and government and the whole diplomatic corps, except those not on speaking terms with the visitor, who are invited but tacitly excused. For visitors the formal ceremony, with band and guard of honour, is repeated on each occasion down to the minutest detail, even to the individuals obliged to leave their warm factory, herded into buses, provided with appropriate flags and ordered to provide a spontaneous popular welcome. The exact repetition of the pattern of welcome has its uses. When President Nixon arrived in Peking, the routine was significantly

varied in order to show that the visit was exceptional and (
not signify the degree of amity normally exhibited to heads
state from the humblest countries.

In new revolutions where head of state means head of sta
and not merely another job between chief sanitary inspect
and head of the stocking industry, it is clearly foolish to be a
sent when he leaves his country or returns to it and expects
full turn-out. It will be noticed and resented if an ambassado
is not there, and the ambassador will get no change out of hin
when next he wants to prevent one of his nationals being sho
for alleged spying. Moreover, a strict observance of local pro
tocol is necessary if the ambassador wants to make a political
point by refusing to appear on an official occasion. It is also
a good rule for a western ambassador never to allow his communist colleagues to outdo him in observance of protocol.
They have probably got a head start on him anyway by pro-
viding a dozen tanks and a free trip to their country.

Successful revolutionaries not subject to the disciplines of the
communist world are apt to treat official ceremonies in accordance with the fancy of the moment. Qasim in Iraq had no
compunction in keeping hundreds of people waiting for two
hours while he expounded to a caller the irrefutable evidence
that he should have Kuwait, and was known to make a two
and a half hours' speech to a large audience on its feet, including ladies, sustained only by one small Coca Cola and – the
majority – by their happy ignorance of Arabic. Heads of state
in the tropics are particularly addicted to ceremony. In Thailand the exhausted, sweating ambassador lives through ten
days of coronation ceremonies in uniform or a morning coat
designed to be worn in London in a cold February wind. An
American ambassador complained to me that the inhabitants
of the Philippines would rather lay a wreath than eat. The
burdens of the ambassador are multiplied if he lives in a capital where the aircraft always arrive in the early hours of the

morning, and it is to Mr Nehru's credit that he ordered that no one should be officially met at the airport between the hours of 8 pm and 8 am. Pity the poor ambassador as he meets the same Soviet officials at the third party on the same afternoon with the conventional greeting, 'Eshchë ras' – 'once more' – or wonders whether he will faint while he waits in a temperature of 100° until the new dictator wakes from his refreshing sleep.

Nine

Domestic Affairs

American embassies used to be and probably still are bound by law to keep their offices open for a specified number of hours a week. In Baghdad at one time they were kept open for twelve hours on Mondays, which enabled the staff to keep reasonable hours for the rest of the week. Diplomatic life is not a nine a.m. to five p.m. job. The staff must be prepared to work at any time seven days a week, especially in countries in which the embassy keeps Sunday as the weekly holiday and everyone else keeps Friday. That sounds stupid, but in fact it gives more trouble if you are out of step with the holidays at home. The ambassador will regard himself as on duty the whole time, inside and outside the office.

It is only too easy for an embassy to become almost exclusively occupied in keeping itself alive. The British diplomatic service, as it is now called, has greatly improved the conditions of life of its members, but like other organs of government in the welfare state, is in danger of becoming over-administered. The head of chancery, who should be primarily responsible for political reporting and the expeditious and secure despatch of business, is likely to find himself spending ninety per cent of his time doing the accounts, filling in forms, writing ever more complicated personnel reports and looking after the junior staff.

Those who have experienced the eccentricities of military administration in the high commission in Germany can happily excuse any defects in the admirable administration of the foreign office, manned by people who know from personal experience all the difficulties which beset a family cast up on an inhospitable foreign shore and who provide so reasonably for the vagrants of the service. In Germany the rations were so precisely divided that even the high commissioner in his vast *Schloss* used to receive his ration of four and a half bananas. Four months after I had asked for a simple wooden bookshelf I was told that it could not be provided, since it was too expensive to provide thirteen, the number of houses in the same road, none of the other occupants of which had asked for one. One day there was delivered to every British house within a radius of forty miles a long looking-glass, a medicine cupboard and a cushion, which had been asked for by one family. It was egalitarianism run mad, the doctrine of the perequation of misery. And we were tightly bound by rank, to a laughable extreme. The visitors' books in the official hostels were spattered with entries such as Mr = Brigadier Smith, since everyone had to have an equivalent military rank to put him in his place. I once even saw Brigadier = Brigadier, presumably inscribed by a retired brigadier employed on the civil side. I believe I was a lieutenant-general, in spite of having with my hearty agreement lost the *Schloss* and Rolls Royce of my predecessor, though I had not achieved this on the way in, when I had to carry the family luggage about a mile down the quay at The Hook because I had not achieved a fictitious rank and the porters were all taken up by the majors. But how scrupulous we were! For our first dinner party our German servants gave us their meat rations and ate ours because they considered it to be below the dignity of the household to serve the old cow steaks which did duty for British rations, while we were not allowed to delve into the German economy.

In my first posting as a young Indian 'civilian', I found an empty house in a hot 'station' in the plains without furniture, curtains, electricity or any household equipment. Nowadays the young Englishman arriving at a foreign post finds a fully furnished flat, with all household equipment and air conditioning in hot climates. There is an administrative staff to look after it all which in the Middle East is engaged in a running battle with the local authorities. After the revolution in Iraq, if the normal channels of business were used, it took six months for a customs clearance to come through, while the goods were stored in the open, being gradually destroyed by rain, sun and white ants. It was said of Turkish offices at the close of the century that 'no private affair receives any attention unless the persons interested continually remind the officials of its existence, request the heads of departments to order the necessary papers to be written, and when the order is obtained, beg some friendly clerk to execute it as a personal favour.'* Experience shows that in the Middle East this is often still the customary procedure. In some posts the embassy may be sure of having its quota of male and female police agents among the local staff. It can be deduced that this happens in the Soviet Union from the fact that the Russians never employ the natives in their embassies abroad. They are cautious people.

In communist countries there is an added administrative complication in normal life resulting from the restriction of the movements of the diplomatic corps to forty kilometres round the capital, their embassies to the capitalists being simi-

* *Turkey in Europe*, by *Odysseus* (Edward Arnold, 1900).

larly restricted in return. I did not find this any hardship in the Soviet Union, since I could get permission to go to far more places than I had the time to visit. Only the service attachés suffered serious restrictions in their movements, which was natural, since their main occupation was to visit places which the Soviet ministry of defence did not want them to see. In communist capitals the ambassador will be well advised always to fly a flag on his car, since, if he does not, grave suspicions will be aroused that he is up to no good.

An ambassador can spend three years in Moscow without ever knowing whether he is being followed. The police probably do not trouble to follow him, knowing that he is a harmless individual who would not be employed on questionable activities. In Iraq after the revolution the local CID, travelling in Volkswagen cars with identifiable number plates and keeping lovingly close to the service attachés, could easily be spotted and were always prepared to relieve their boredom on our partridge shoots by helping to look for lost birds. During my time in Egypt I was normally accompanied by a car provided with a full complement of armed policemen to protect me from Nasser's enemies, who might attack me in order to get him into trouble, and presumably to report where I went and whom I saw. When I walked across the road to visit my American colleague, they surrounded me. I used to name them coverpoint, square leg and mid-off. They watched me playing tennis – an unprofitable occupation – and rode behind me on the desert, though they forebore to climb the great pyramid and the cavalry disappeared in the desert, as soon as it was out of sight of the police station. Great pleasure of an ornithological kind may be had in the observation of the habits of the local police. In countries in which the ambassador is accustomed to these little attentions, he must get used with difficulty, on return to his own country, to not having the delicate and assiduous attention of so many employees of foreign governments. He is no longer of the slightest importance to anyone.

Embassy administration in communist countries is also complicated by the game of mutual expulsion which demands some skill in the playing. If you can afford a large embassy in the other capital, you have more men on the board to be taken than the other government has in your capital, and therefore have an initial advantage. A secretary is expelled for alleged improper activities. An official of similar rank is expelled by the other side on similar grounds. According to the rules, you cannot get a bishop for a pawn. But within the limits of rank, the retaliating government will be able to get rid of the man who is thought to be most troublesome but has not been caught out, so that it may end up with the advantage of the exchange.

The communists have the advantage that all the business done in a capitalist country by private firms, exports, shipping, insurance, tourism and so on, is done under their system by government officials; they therefore have a far larger pack into which to insert some jokers and from which to lose a few cards. But there is a point at which this superiority becomes too great for the other side to suffer. It then discards the rule-book and throws out a ship-full. This puts the side losing its men in a dilemma. If it throws out an equal amount, the smaller embassy will have no one left, which will escalate the game of expulsion until neither side has an embassy. The political consequences of this would be such that it is not in the interest of either side to go so far; so the retaliation will be limited to a few people in the corresponding embassy, though the number can be swollen for public effect by the addition of some names of former members of the embassy, picked at random, and a few businessmen thrown in for good measure. The two sides then settle down to mutual recrimination and insult and to mutual refusal of visas and of normal diplomatic contacts, until they get tired of the affair and return gradually to normal.

DOMESTIC AFFAIRS

All ambassadors have a running battle with that section of the department of the environment which used to be called the ministry of works. This provides a salutary counter-irritant, which absorbs all the surplus emotion of the ambassador generated by his political and personal problems. The ambassador protests that the new furniture makes his drawing-room look like the front parlour of a brothel, that his office would be more suitable for a couturier in Buenos Aires, that the chairs for the staff flats, received after a two and a half year delay, collapse when the occupants sit on them. In Cairo the new British chancery designed soon after the Festival of Britain, with every wall flaunting a different colour and ostentatious reproductions of the royal arms picked out in white on the front of the ambassador's desk, was known locally as 'by South Bank out of Great West Road'. The decorations were reluctantly modified on my protest.

There is however another side to the picture. The post of the ministry's local supervisor is well in the danger zone: its occupant is a long-suffering man. The new ambassador's wife inevitably has tastes different from her predecessor's. The Nasmyths and the reproduction regency chairs go back into the store-room and are replaced by the latest productions of Messrs Heal and the Marlborough Gallery. With the next incumbent the process is reversed. The much harried supervisor consoles himself by having the best furnished flat in the embassy.

To any embassy the most important migrant, more important than a visiting minister, is the inspector. He stays virtuously and uncomfortably in a hotel, so that he should not be corrupted by hospitality. He retires into his shell for several weeks with his slide-rule and the evidence provided by everyone in the embassy, conclusively proving that they are incredibly poor and that the proper performance of their duties requires them to mortgage the old family home and refuse all aid to their starving widowed mother and sisters. In the end he

comes to the surface and presents an incomprehensible calculation showing, according to his temperament, that everyone in
the embassy should have their allowances either doubled or
halved. Since human beings remember only bad news, the
general impression is that he tends towards the latter answer
to his sums.

British inspectors, having cut your allowances in half,
used to give a little relief by applying the curious treasury rule
that everyone in an embassy had a putative child of eight who
had to be clothed and fed, which was especially welcome to
those who had no children in that category. There is nothing
that can be done about the inspector except to treat him as a
visitation of nature like a plague of locusts or a cooling rain after
drought in accordance with his findings. It is safer to tell all,
since he invariably finds out if you withhold information, and
prudent to feed him badly once or twice in order to show that
you cannot afford anything better. The ambassador will seek
to advance the inspector's visit if he believes the embassy to be
badly off and the designated inspector has the reputation of
being of a kindly and generous disposition, and to delay it if
he foresees cuts, or if the current inspector is known to be
jaundiced and mean.

The central ceremony of embassy life is the ritual of the
diplomatic bag. It is an expensive and complicated operation.
Someone buried in a London attic tenuously connected with
the Foreign Office takes a hundred retired service officers –
or whatever the number is – pours in a bag of airline schedules,
stirs vigorously and allows the mixture to simmer gently till
ready. Enormous ingenuity is shown in routing the Queen's
messengers so as to cover the largest number of posts with the
smallest number of colonels. In sensitive areas they travel in
pairs so as to avoid being raped on the way. The rhythm of
embassy life centres on the bag and it is advisable for outsiders
to give the embassy a wide berth on bag day, especially when

the schedule is disrupted by the vagaries of the weather or the airlines. It is not advisable, though not unknown, for an ambassador to use his diplomatic bag to enhance his salary by conducting profitable and illegal currency deals, or selling duty-free cigarettes on the black market. It is even suspected that some governments encourage these habits in their ambassadors in order to be able to economise on their emoluments. But the British are not guilty of these peccadilloes. A British head of chancery guards the virginity of his bag like a mid-Victorian chaperon at an attractive maiden's first ball.

One of the ambassador's most tiresome problems is how to ensure that he is sent young members of the service with a capacity for logical thought. He needs them to do his thinking for him, since it is probable that by the time he has become a senior ambassador he will have ceased to be able to think for himself. A whole treatise could be written on the form of Chinese shadow boxing which regulates the exchanges between a British ambassador and the personnel department of the foreign office. The department's letters must be dissected and interpreted like an important pronouncement of the communist party of the Soviet Union, since they are invariably replete with hidden meanings. To be successful, the head of the personnel department must acquire the delicate art of forcing a card on the suspicious ambassador, without afterwards exposing himself to reproaches that the card did not respond to specifications. The ambassador, on his side, must acquire the even more delicate art of discarding a card, without wholly alienating the sympathies of the head of the personnel department. Occasionally he has to take the two of clubs in order to get a court card as compensation. The personnel department has a number of standard and easily recognisable moves in the game. The most ominous signal is when they write that you have done so well in an exceptionally difficult post that you should have a well-deserved rest before taking up another post of greater responsibility. This means that they realise that they cannot leave you much longer where you are, but have not the faintest idea what to do with you next. After some years in the post, a head of the personnel department has to train himself to think straight again.

Embassies are tightly knit little communities, especially where the staff live and work on top of each other. It matters far more than at home how the boss and his wife treat the staff and how the staff look on them. The very few ambassadors and their wives who have an inflated sense of their own importance have it in their power to make life miserable for their staffs. The British foreign service used to have its own folklore on this subject. There was the ambassador's wife who liked to catch out a nervous young wife without hat and gloves at a function at which the ambassador's wife was wearing them. There was the embassy where it was understood that whatever family, social or domestic emergency might occur, the ambassador's wife came first and that the wife who did not conform to this simple rule was ruining her husband's career. When the nanny had given notice, the baby was cutting its teeth and the cook was on holiday, the young couple would be required to fill a gap in an embassy lunch party at ten minutes' notice or to be at the airport complete with hat and gloves at midday in the tropics to meet the ambassador and his wife returning from a few days' tour in the country.

There was the curious custom, which used to be widely practised, by which at every party at which the ambassador and his wife were present, members of the staff were expected to be there before them and to leave after them, so that by three a.m., if the ambassador liked dancing, every pillar was draped with exhausted members of his staff longing to go home. There were the embassies where the staff were used as unpaid guides or to give dinner parties for the ambassador's private guests who were staying too long, and those where the staff were never invited into the house at all, which saved the 'frais' and preserved the statistics of entertainment of foreigners.

The folklore collected only the few exceptions to the happy relations normally found in British embassies abroad. And when the junior staff were treated sympathetically by the ambassador and his wife, it was reasonable that they should reciprocate and not turn up at embassy parties after all the guests had arrived, looking like something which the police had picked up on a Saturday night in Cable Street. There were only a few of those too, and most of the staff responded to an ambassador's wife who looked after them and had consideration for them, who treated everyone naturally and alike, and who suffered without flinching and with charm all the social duties, the domestic difficulties and the guests who regarded the hospitality of the embassy as due to them by right to save them the expense of a hotel.

The degree of essentiality of any member of an embassy is in inverse proportion to his or her rank in it. If the ambassador is withdrawn for political reasons, there is not a ripple; no one notices it. If the head of chancery is removed, a young secretary happily takes his place. But if the girl secretaries or the maintenance engineer should go on strike, the machine would stop at once. The chancery guards who alone know at what time the ambassador's daughter comes home, the archivist who preserves every scrap of paper with great care and then burns it all, the ambassador's personal assistant who, when not feeding her cat, has it in her power to make the place a haven of peace or a jangling of frayed tempers, the young men in chancery who consider themselves far more intelligent than the ambassador, but who tolerate him owing to his power over their future careers, the ubiquitous dragoman, by whatever name he goes, that infinitely valuable person who stays in one place for ever, knows everybody and has a far greater influence than the temporary tenant of the ambassador's house, the attachés, civil and service, going independently about their business and having only a tenuous connection with the rest of the embassy, the minister (not to be confused with the ambassador's master at home or the chaplain), urging the ambassador to go on leave so that he can hold charge – the list can be long in a large embassy, often too long. We have gone a long way from the day when the ambassador chose his butler, his cook and his secretary to accompany him. Perhaps we should do better in many embassies to revert to the old system.

Ten

The View Towards Home

The British ambassador ruminates on the new foreign secretary. Foreign secretaries are great people, altogether in a class above mere officials. They are Olympians, gods whose ways are not to be understood by mere officials, and are beset by Olympian problems from which the officials are mercifully free. But the ambassador, having probably received an old-fashioned classical education, has become imbued with the Greek habit of not taking the gods too seriously and of discoursing upon their more wayward habits rather than upon their innate perfection. It must not be assumed that he takes a cynical or superior view of these great persons. Far from it; he knows who is the boss, is loyal to him and respects him. He may therefore be allowed, in the privacy of his own study, to observe the species in a zoological sort of way, while the underlying respect may be taken for granted.

The ambassador has an ingrained scepticism on the subject of new foreign secretaries; they change so rapidly in British political practice that there always seems to be a new man to break in. Some foreign ministers have spent half their lives at the game and know all the moves. It can at least be hoped that the new man can absorb his brief and not get hit all over the ground by the old professionals. On his first day of office he has found his way, with a little help from the office messengers who have done it so often before, to his large ornate office, cast an abstracted eye on the pelicans in St James's Park, undertaken the ritual act of moving his desk and changing a picture or two, in order to show that he is an innovator, not bound by his predecessor's obsolete policy, and wonders how he can keep his end up in the face of all those glossy, superior, hypercritical young men in the private office, racing up the ladder of promotion or completing their education in the stimulating atmosphere of great affairs, on their way to a more profitable haven in the City.

He is bound to start by feeling that he cannot just sit back and do nothing and must show himself to be forceful and active in the Palmerston tradition. He will be tempted to act as if Britain were still a major world power on the same level as the two super-powers, and may be misled by the impact of the large and efficient machine at his command, at home and overseas, which generates the hundreds of telegrams pouring onto his desk and the taut, pungent 'minutes' on the situation from Kamskatchka to Peru, by the proliferation of questions on foreign affairs from keen young members of parliament wrapped in the illusion of power, and by the rows of foreign ambassadors demanding audience in order to keep up their prestige at home.

He will do much better if he has no ambition to make his name in the post and is content to keep quiet until the moment comes when he must intervene and can do so effectively. He cannot look forward to gaining a personal success in his term of office. Opportunities for diplomatic feats like Anthony

Eden's achievements at the Geneva conference on South-East Asia in 1954 and in the creation of the Western European Union on the ruins of the European Defence Community, will only rarely come to a foreign secretary in the present world situation. Moreover Eden's laurels looked a little dusty after Suez and those years are likely to be known as the time of Britain's missed opportunities in Europe. In foreign affairs, with persistence and patience over a long period, a situation can sometimes be improved; but though you can lose sensationally, you never seem to win. Of course he will learn what it is all about in time, but there will then be another round of musical chairs and he will find himself back in the department of sealing wax and sewage disposal.

The office will soon find out whether he has no principles or too many. The clever opportunist has the advantage of a mind unencumbered by prejudice, but a modest ration of principles is desirable. When they are tempered by a realism painfully acquired by experience, the amalgam is generally considered the more satisfactory product for home consumption and export. It is to be hoped that he does not see the world solely in terms of good and evil, whether the evil is communism, nationalism, the United Nations committee on colonial affairs or the government which is at the moment most troublesome to British ideas of how the world ought to be governed. For some years General de Gaulle and President Nasser were generally at the head of the unpopularity stakes, because it was subconsciously felt that they ought to adapt their interests to ours, while the Soviet and Chinese leaders did not arouse anything like the same degree of heat, since they were expected to be unpleasant anyway and anything short of complete unpleasantness was marked up to their credit.

It is even more to be deplored if he should see foreign affairs principally in terms of the good of his party and of his own position in it, and limit his vision to nine days ahead during the session, the period for which House of Commons business is fixed, and when the House is not sitting, to the duration of the recess or the interval until the next party conference. Of course it is true, as Monsieur Reynaud remarked, that 'in the eyes of our British friends, first of all comes the House of Commons and then nothing, and after that nothing again, and then comes God: and the idea of inserting some kind of authority between the House of Commons and the Almighty seems to them something very like sacrilege'.* But to the ambassador called home for consultations there is no greater relief than to find out for himself that a new foreign secretary assesses the problems of foreign affairs objectively and that his judgement is not swayed either by ideology or by politics at home.

In the tradition of my time, the memory of Ernest Bevin was outstanding. He was a man loved by all who worked for him, genuine, honest and full of courage. 'Minutes' for him had to be kept to one side of one sheet of paper. It was an admirable lesson in concentration of thought. He wrote perhaps two illegible words, which were translated by the private secretary, specially trained for the purpose, but they always made sense, and in my brief experience in the foreign office under him, always showed his sure political instinct and judgement. Everyone knew that if he said 'I won't 'ave it' in the cabinet, he got his way, and this gave him a very strong position. Alas! Like so many great men, he did not know when to leave, and his last years of office showed a painful deterioration in his powers.

Mr Khruschchev once told me that he thought Anthony Eden the best of our politicians, but added that he did not know what had happened to him in the end. At his best Anthony Eden was in the top world class. He was in his best form during the Geneva conference of 1954 on South-East Asia. The communists were sweeping across Indo-China; Mr Dulles

* Quoted by Professor Beloff in *Foreign Policy and the Diplomatic Process*

was trying to commit him to joint intervention and would not talk to the Chinese, who were suspicious of everyone in their first international conference after the revolution. The French Government fell in the middle of the conference. Yet agreement was reached and the fighting was stopped. Much credit was due to Monsieur Mendès France, but without Eden the conference would, I believe, have altogether failed. And if the opportunities for peace in Indo-China given by that conference were not pursued, that was not the fault of those who brought about at least a breathing-space in the troubles of that unhappy land. It is right to remember a statesman by his best achievements and not only by his failures.

If the new foreign secretary wants to reform the office, he will find it difficult to do much more than change the cup of tea at the desk to a whisky and soda on the sofa, or move the position of the recommendation in a 'minute' from front to rear or rear to front, opposite to whichever it happened to be before. If the last man stayed at home, will he see an urgent need for personal consultations with foreign statesmen as the only effective method of conducting foreign affairs? If the last man travelled, will he feel it his duty to remain on the bridge and keep his hand on the helm? What will be his personal relations with the office? If he is a large landed proprietor, they will come easy to him. He will treat the permanent under secretary like his factor, the assistant under secretaries like his farmers on a day with the hounds and the heads of department like his gamekeeper. The private secretary will rank high, like his trainer, the assistant private secretaries like his jockeys. It will all be very natural. If he has not been born with a Georgian silver spoon in his mouth, he may be suspicious that they are all reactionary members of the 'establishment', bent on obstructing his progressive policy. It will take him only a short time to realise that nowadays the 'establishment' is to be found on the farm, in a photographer's studio or in a merchant bank, and that the members of the diplomatic service are mostly men with a mental equipment above the average from average middle class families, with a sprinkling of the upper and lower crusts, who will be loyal to him if he is loyal to them, supports the service in public and defends it against the attacks of his colleagues and the treasury.

If he has a quick brain, an open mind and a sense of history, if he has good judgement of men, a sure touch and an instinct for diplomacy, if, whatever his former profession, he is not by temperament a lawyer or a missionary, if he has the courage to take politically unpopular decisions and the thick skin which he should have acquired in political life and does not easily lose his nerve or his sleep, if policy is conducted on his side of Downing Street, he will be rated by those critical, intelligent young men round him as somewhere near the top of the tree. But he will probably not stay long enough to make a real impression before his virtues and failings pass into history and the new man enters with springy nervous step and starts changing the pictures again.

The ambassador trusts that the foreign secretary, besides contemplating the pelicans in St James's park, will give a little time to clearing his mind on the principles of British foreign policy, before he becomes immersed in the flood of paper. He will, of course, start from the premise that British policy should serve British interests. This is not a purely selfish concept. It is a British interest, for instance, that the peace should be secure, that the strong should not gobble up the weak, that international disputes, even if they cannot be settled, should at least be talked over until the danger point has passed, that atomic weapons should not get into the hands of any country which might be tempted to use them and that the nuclear balance should be maintained, that relations between the capitalist and communist countries should become gradually easier, that the developing countries should be able to raise the living standards of their people, that governments should keep their word, in particular their treaties and other international engagements, so long as it is in their power to do so, and that they should generally observe the principles of international law.

Policy, like babies, used to be made casually, in response to immediate urges or needs. Now everything, from families to foreign policy, is planned. A planning section has been created in the foreign office, which has shed its old suspicion of anything savouring of the academic approach or any attempt to speculate on hypothetical situations. Of course, owing to the vagaries of human behaviour, the plans are not always carried out. The planners must reconcile themselves to seeing them dented or distorted by violent contact with domestic politics or acts of God, dictators or revolutionaries, or by discoveries by the scientists in their ivory towers, producing from their retorts and test-tubes cataclysmic transformations of the world scene. But it is a decided improvement in method that serious thought is now not limited to problems demanding immediate solution, but is also applied to surveying the future changes and chances of this fleeting world and of British interests in it.

Policy should be formed on a clear understanding of the world as it is and on an objective assessment of the balance of political, military and economic forces, not on sentimental recollections of a vanished past. It should be a policy which we can afford, and which we can back up effectively by the economic and military power which we and our allies can apply to a particular situation. It should not be distorted by irrelevant pressures such as a domestic struggle to acquire or retain political power, but must be such as to command the support of informed British public opinion and of the majority in parliament. No issue of foreign policy can be considered in isolation. Each question must be considered in the light of its influence on other questions and relationships and of their influence on it. Lord Strang wrote that 'one of Bevin's great qualities was his sense of international relationship. For him no matter of foreign policy ever stood alone.' I remember Bevin expounding to Field Marshal Smuts how he believed that no foreign secretary had ever had to keep so many balls in the air at the same time. Finally, there is never a correct answer to any problem of foreign policy. The maker of policy can only choose what appears to be the least disadvantageous course open to him.

It is all very elementary stated in this way, just a series of clichés. But these elementary principles are often disregarded with disastrous results. The communist and anti-communist crusades have led powerful countries on both sides of the ideological curtain into unnecessary troubles. The British have gone woefully wrong by adopting policies which would have been successful when Britain was relatively more powerful, but which had no chance of success when her position in the world had weakened. The super-powers have both over-extended themselves by a forward policy in areas in which they could not apply sufficient strength to back it up or in which the adverse political forces were too strong to be overcome. New revolutionary régimes have been too ambitious from over-estimating their strength and from believing that having made a successful revolution in their own country, they could repeat it in others. The principles which should govern foreign affairs are clear enough, but at the moment of decision, emotion and ambition are sometimes stronger than rational thought. And if you hear a foreign minister declaring piously that his policy is based on moral principles, you may be sure that he is deceiving you and perhaps himself too.

The new foreign secretary no longer has the advantages or the responsibilities of a power of the first rank, but is enmeshed in an immense variety of complex relationships. He is confronted by struggles of ideologies and nationalisms and by all the complications arising from political instability and racial jealousies in a host of new states having leaders with little political experience and an uncertain political base. He will reflect that there have been few periods of British history when Britain could act effectively on the world stage without allies. He must resist the temptation to overplay his hand, but must use every bit of influence which the country inherits from the past, and which it can still exercise effectively in spite of its relative loss of power. It is, in the main, an ungrateful task before him and he knows he will be lucky if he comes out of it with his political reputation unimpaired.

The ambassador sighs and turns to the immediate task of seeing how he can persuade his keenest young secretary, without discouraging him, that a twelve page dissertation on a more than usually abstruse subject of no great political import, is rather more than he can expect a busy minister to read. And it is time to take the dog for a walk.

Index

INDEX